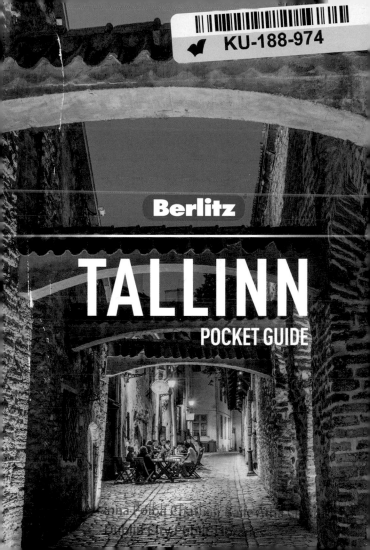

Berlitz

TALLINN

POCKET GUIDE

Walking Eye
mobile app

Discover the world's best destinations with the Insight Guides Walking Eye app, available to download for free in the App Store and Google Play.

The container app provides easy access to fantastic free content on events and activities taking place in your current location or chosen destination, with the possibility of booking, as well as the regularly-updated Insight Guides travel blog: Inspire Me. In addition, you can purchase curated, premium destination guides through the app, which feature local highlights, hotel, bar, restaurant and shopping listings, an A to Z of practical information and more. Or purchase and download Insight Guides eBooks straight to your device.

TOP 10 ATTRACTIONS

TOOMPEA CASTLE
From the 13th century onwards this was the historic seat of power in Estonia. See page 31.

DOME CHURCH
Great architecture and a turbulent history characterise Tallinn's grand Lutheran cathedral. See page 35.

TOOMPEA'S VIEWING PLATFORMS
Enjoy a fairy-tale panorama. See page 36.

THE TOWN HALL
Fine medieval woodcarvings are among its treasures. See page 40.

HOLY SPIRIT CHURCH
Its eye-catching clock has been ticking since the 1600s. See page 42.

SEAPLANE HARBOUR
Explore the vast maritime museum and historic ships. See page 59.

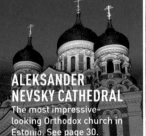

ALEKSANDER NEVSKY CATHEDRAL
The most impressive-looking Orthodox church in Estonia. See page 30.

KUMU
The soul of the nation comes to light at Tallinn's grandest art museum. See page 64.

TOWN HALL SQUARE
Once Tallinn's main marketplace, this is still the life and soul of the Old Town. See page 39.

KADRIORG PALACE
Peter the Great's summer residence is a reminder of imperial Russia. See page 61.

A PERFECT DAY

9.00am

Breakfast

Get your energy fix with a breakfast of sausages and herring in your hotel, or grab a coffee and pastry in the Town Hall's medieval-style corner café. On Town Hall Square, find the Centre of Tallinn stone and see how far you have to stretch to spot the five towers.

9.30am

Toompea climb

Make a leisurely ascent up Pikk jalg to catch a glimpse of Aleksander Nevsky Cathedral's onion domes in the morning light, then beat the crowds to the viewing platforms for snapshots of Old Town rooftops.

12.30pm

Retail therapy

Head to St Catherine's Passage and wind your way through the craft workshops to watch the artists at work. Pour through the wares at the Sweater Wall to find an authentic souvenir. If you're hungry, grab a bite at Controvento (see page 106) or one of the restaurants on Vene Street.

10.30am

Old Town

Navigate your way through the cobblestone streets of Lower Town and see how many colourful doorways you can find. Stop in at the Great Guild Hall at Pikk 17 or the Tallinn City Museum on Vene 17 for deeper historic insights.

2pm

Kadriorg

Catch tram No. 1 to Kadriorg Park, stroll around the pathways, feed the ducks at the Swan Pond and inspect the manicured flowerbeds behind the Kadriorg Palace. Time permitting, take the path to the Russalka Memorial and gaze out over Tallinn Bay.

IN TALLINN

6pm

Historic dining

Make your way back towards Old Town by tram, or by walking along Narva road to see the city's contemporary edge. If you have the power, make a detour to the Radisson BLU Hotel at Rävala 3 to catch the views from its 24th floor café. Satisfy the hunger you've worked up in the city's famed medieval restaurant, Olde Hansa, or its equally lively neighbour Peppersack (see page 109), both of which are built into beautiful, Hanseatic-era houses.

11pm

Nightcap

Wind the evening down with a final beer, glass of wine or shot of Vana Tallinn at one of the city's elegant wine bars, or make your way to Clayhills Gastropub (*Pikk 13*) for live music.

3.30pm

Culture fix

Make contact with your creative side by visiting any or all of the art museums of Kadriorg – the palace itself with its foreign art collection, the Mikkel with its exquisite porcelain, and the vast, modern Kumu, Estonia's award-winning national gallery.

8pm

Bar-hopping

Take in the night-time ambience of the square as its terraces begin to fill with revellers, then head to Suur-Karja and Väike-Karja to begin your tour of the area's bars, picking the ones with the oddest themes. The underground Karja Kelder (Väike Karja 1) has the most local flavour and is a good place to try various Estonian beers, while Nimeta (Suur-Karja 4) is a guaranteed party spot for the international crowd.

CONTENTS

INTRODUCTION

Steeped in history, pulsing with energy and beaming with fairy-tale charm, Tallinn has earned its place among the must-see destinations of Europe. The city's soul is equally fed by a progressive arts scene, the natural beauty of its parks and coastline, a buzzing nightlife and a post-Soviet edginess. All this, and the fact that it can be toured by foot, make Tallinn an ideal choice for a city break.

This cosy city of just 450,000 inhabitants on the southern shore of the Gulf of Finland occupies an enviable position as a regional gateway. Its nearest neighbour, Helsinki, is only 90 minutes away by ship, and Stockholm and St Petersburg can both be reached by overnight ferry. Latvia's capital, Riga, is a five-hour bus ride away.

Tallinn's role as a port-of-call is nothing new. In fact, that has been the city's defining feature since the early 13th century when Danish troops and German crusaders invaded Estonia and laid the foundations of a major commercial hub. Soon after, Tallinn became a member of the Hanseatic League, an all-important association of merchant cities during medieval times. It grew rich in the 14th and 15th centuries as the middleman in trade between the West and Novgorod in Russia. In the centuries that followed, the Swedish empire, the Russian empire and the Soviet Union each conquered this desirable port city, making their own intriguing contributions to Tallinn's urban landscape.

A MEDIEVAL MILIEU, A MODERN EDGE

Without question, Tallinn's most valuable treasure is its Old Town – a remarkable survivor from the Middle Ages. Encircled by a centuries-old city wall, this is a beguiling place of narrow streets and intimate squares, ancient houses and towering church spires. Like no other place in Europe, this area has somehow managed to hang on to its medieval atmosphere despite centuries of commerce, war and political change. The neighbourhood owes much of its survival to a series of historic accidents. Economic downturns kept construction in check, and at critical junctures, shrewd political settlements prevented the town from being sacked. The city's famous defensive

The town hall tower in the heart of Tallinn's old town

wall, most of which is still intact, also helped a great deal in preserving the town for future generations. The area suffered from Soviet bombing towards the end of World War II, and from some dubious reconstruction that followed, but the ensuing occupation also had at least one unexpected benefit: trapped as it was in the amber of the Soviet Union, Tallinn's Old Town escaped the overdevelopment inflicted on similar cities in the West. Now for the most part restored to its original glory, the Old Town once again belongs to the world; it has been inscribed on Unesco's list of World Heritage Sites.

But do not think of the Old Town as a static museum piece – it is nothing of the kind. This is the heart of Tallinn, the hub of its busy and eclectic restaurant scene and home to the city's famously raucous nightlife. Scattered amid the 15th-century buildings are trendy cafés, nearly all of them offering Wi-fi so that iPad-wielding locals can stay connected with the world. Town

Hall Square, at the centre of the Old Town, is home to countless concerts, festivals and other performances. Bustling markets fill the streets, mingling with crowds of foreign visitors, all of whom add their own energy to the mix. And shopping here knows no limits. In short, as ironic as it sounds, the Old Town is where the heart of modern Tallinn beats the strongest.

This captivating part of town usually keeps visitors exploring for days, because there is always a new detail to see each time you meander through the same street. As much as there is to see in the Old Town, limiting yourself to this area would be a crime. Within the city limits you can see the spectacular Kadriorg Palace, built for Russian Tsar Peter the Great, the museum ships of Seaplane Harbour, the beautiful Pirita beach and river area, the re-created farm villages in the Estonian Open Air Museum and some curious, Soviet-era constructions on the outskirts of town. Also, a number of relatively undiscovered cities not far from Tallinn offer fantastic day-trip opportunities.

PEOPLE AND ECONOMY

'Eastern Europe' this is not. While lumped in with its Slavic and Baltic neighbours by virtue of having been caught on the wrong side of the Iron Curtain, Estonia sees itself as having much more in common with Nordic countries. Indeed, the country's language and ethnic roots are Finno-Ugric, closely related to their cousins, the Finns. Maybe it is not surprising then that Estonians, like the Scandinavians and the Finns, tend to be serious, hard-working people, with a somewhat stoic manner.

Booze cruisers

Tallinn is a popular destination for Finnish shoppers, particularly those after cheap deals on alcohol, which is heavily taxed in Finland.

The fortified gateway to Tallinn's bustling historic district

They are less gregarious and less likely to laugh than Spanish or Italians, but it does not mean they don't get the joke.

They are also a people whose desire for self-determination runs deep. Perhaps that is why, after regaining independence in 1991, they were so quick to dust off a half-century of Soviet grey and rapidly catch up, economically and culturally, with the rest of Europe. Signs of the economic boom that the country experienced after it joined the European Union in 2004 are clearly visible in the shopping malls and high-rise hotels that dot the downtown area. However, that boom, long-since tapered off, was not enough to prevent an outflow of construction workers and medical staff seeking higher wages in Finland – something that continues to trouble the economy.

On the more positive side of Estonia's recent development is its transformation into an 'e-society', where the locals' love of all things high-tech has given rise to a huge array of online

Tech-savvy Tallinn

Tallinn consistently rates as one of the most high-tech cities in Europe, and the country itself has been dubbed e-Estonia. In 2000, Estonia became the first country to declare Internet access to be a human right.

government services and commercial applications. This is the city where Skype was invented in 2003, where a citywide Wi-fi network was rolled out more than 15 years ago and where trials of a high-tech delivery robot named Starship were kick-started in 2017. At the start of 2018, Estonia also became one of the first nations with 5G network capability.

For the visitor, this forward-looking attitude adds up to a convenient, comfortable stay. Online booking, free Wi-fi and fluency in English are all the norm.

SEASONS

Tallinn's extreme climate means it is a highly seasonal city, as far as tourism – or anything else – goes. During the short period of warm weather, usually May to August, flocks of cruise-ship passengers and other visitors descend on the Old Town, filling the restaurants and hotel rooms. Still, this is the best time to visit, with the weather at its friendliest, festivals and concerts easiest to find, and the city generally at its most vibrant. That said, a visit in the off-season is perfectly reasonable for anyone who wants to avoid the crowds. There will still be plenty to see and do, even when outdoor cafés are no longer an option, and you will have the enchanting medieval streets almost to yourself. A visit during winter, provided you are dressed properly for it, can be a truly magical experience as the snow blankets the tiled rooftops and the town turns on its Christmas charm.

A BRIEF HISTORY

A quick glance at Tallinn's history will leave no doubt as to why locals are so fiercely passionate about their independence. For nearly all of the past eight centuries their nation has been ruled by foreign powers, starting with subjugation by the Danish crown, then German crusaders, the Polish-Lithuanian Commonwealth, the Swedish empire, the Russian empire and, most recently, the Soviet Union. It is fairly remarkable that, against these odds, the Estonians have been able to hang on to their language and cultural identity through the years.

The secret to their resilience might be that their roots run incredibly deep. While historians argue about just exactly when

Aleksander Nevsky Cathedral on Toompea

the ancestors of the ancient Eesti (or 'Aestii' as the Romans may have called them) arrived on the Baltic coast, most put the date some time between 8000 and 3000BC.

Little is known about the pre-Christian period of Estonia's history, but archaeological evidence suggests that in the years before the arrival of the first invaders, the northern Estonian Rävala people lived a clan-like existence, engaged in farming, fishing and, increasingly, trade with their Baltic Sea neighbours. By the 12th century AD, they had built a wooden fortress on Toompea hill, which the Arab cartographer Abu Abdallah Muhammed al-Idrisi marked on his world map in 1154 as a 'seasonal stronghold'. This was the first mention of Tallinn, or at least its precursor, in historical records.

FIRST INVADERS

In the early 13th century, the Pope's call for a crusade against the pagan peoples around the Baltic Sea prompted a bloody and complicated struggle between Swedes, Danes, Russians, German crusaders and local tribes. As part of this land grab, King Valdemar II of Denmark conquered the Estonians' stronghold on Toompea in 1219, immediately replacing it with his own fortress and subjugating northern Estonia. Valdemar's victory was a key turning point in Estonia's history, marking the beginning of a long period of foreign rule, with Toompea, the hill at the centre of Tallinn, always the regional seat of power.

German crusaders had meantime gained a foothold in Riga and were battling their way northward. In 1227, their military arm, the Order of the Brothers of the Sword, occupied Toompea and gained control of the Danish holdings. A papal decree returned power to the Danes in 1238, by which time a feudal system, with Germans as landlords, had been instituted in the countryside. More significantly for the development of Tallinn, the Order had invited 200 German merchant families to settle at the foot of Toompea hill, thereby sowing the seeds of a commercial capital. For the next 700 years, the descendants of these 'Baltic Germans' remained the dominant class both in the country and in the city.

A CITY BUILT ON SALT

Tallinn's true heyday came in the 13th–16th centuries when it flourished as a major trading port on the route between East and West. This development into a booming merchant centre was kicked off in 1248, when the Danish king allowed Tallinn to adopt Lübeck Law, effectively making it a self-ruling city-state. What's more, around 1284 the city became a

The Middle Ages

When Tallinn city was enclosed by a wall, it did not include Toompea, home to the Baltic German nobility and base for Estonia's foreign rulers. Tension between Tallinn and Toompea was fuelled by a city law that allowed any runaway peasant who managed to stay within the town walls for a year and a day to be declared free of his master, providing the city with much-needed labour. Tallinn and Toompea remained separate, and often at odds, until they were officially united in the late 1880s.

member of the Hanseatic League, a powerful association of cities that held a monopoly over northern European trade.

As the key Hansa port dealing with trade to Russia, Tallinn was a guaranteed success. Russian fur and wax, and Estonian grain and linen, were exported to cities in Western Europe, while textiles, herring, wine and spices went in the opposite direction. The most valuable commodity that came through Tallinn, however, was salt, said to be worth its weight in gold at the time. In fact, so much profitable salt cargo changed hands here on its way east that Tallinn became known as a city 'built on salt'.

It was during the boom years of the 1300s and 1400s that most of the present-day Old Town took shape. The city wall and towers

◌ THE MANY NAMES OF TALLINN

Tallinn's oldest recorded name is Qaleveni, as Arab cartographer al-Idrisi marked on his world map in 1154. Old Russian chronicles used the somewhat similar Kolyvan, while Scandinavians probably referred to the city as Lindanise or Lindana. From the Middle Ages to the early 20th century, the ruling ethnic German elite used the name Reval (or Rewel), as the city was at the centre of the ancient Rävala county.

Estonians, however, called it Tallinn. The name originates from the period of Danish rule (1219–1346) when the city was referred to as *Castrum Danorum* (Danish Castle), which in Estonian was *tannin lidna*. Another theory is that the name comes from a fusion of *Taani* (Danish) and *linn* (city), which first became Taanilinna and later Tallinn. After independence in 1918, the capital's official name was changed from Reval to Tallinn, but in 1925 the variation Tallinna was adopted. Finally, in 1933, it was changed back to Tallinn.

were built and improved, workshops and warehouses sprung up, and a new Town Hall was installed in 1404 to house the City Council, the all-powerful body that controlled town life and international trade.

In 1346, Toompea's tenants changed. After the Estonians led a massive, but unsuccessful revolt called the St George's Night Uprising (1343–5), Denmark, which was then having its own internal difficulties, sold northern Estonia to the Riga-based German knights. Thus all of Estonia came under the control of the Livonian Order, which already ruled southern Estonia and present-day Latvia. In independent Tallinn however, the political changeover had little impact.

Sixteenth-century suit of armour, Kiek in de Kök

FROM EMPIRE TO EMPIRE

Fortunes changed drastically in the mid-16th century with the outbreak of the Livonian War (1558–83). By now the Livonian state was in decline and, smelling blood, Russia, Sweden, the Polish-Lithuanian Commonwealth and Denmark all moved in for a share of the Baltic stakes. Tallinn and the nobles on Toompea negotiated surrender with Sweden in 1561, but the costly war would continue for two more decades.

The ensuing 'Swedish Period' of the nation's history is characterised by enlightened social policies, including more rights for peasants and the establishment of the nation's education system. But in the city itself, the situation had greatly deteriorated. Post-war plagues and famines caused Tallinn's population to plummet, and the city's role as a trade gateway to Russia had been taken over by competitors. The boom times were clearly over.

Conflict broke out again in the early 18th century, this time with imperial Sweden and an expansionist Russia fighting over Baltic territories in the devastating Great Northern War (1700–21). In 1710 Tsar Peter the Great captured Tallinn from the Swedes, and Estonia became a province of the Russian empire. Estonian peasants lost the privileges they had gained under Swedish rule and were forced into the same slave-like serfdom practised in the rest of tsarist Russia.

NATIONAL AWAKENING

The 19th century, by contrast, brought huge improvements for ethnic Estonians. Serfdom was abolished in 1816, and from 1860 to 1880 a cultural revival referred to as the 'National Awakening' reached its height. Societies of 'Estophiles' promoted Estonian literature and culture, previously considered of little value. Estonian poetry bloomed, Estonian-language newspapers appeared, and the famous national epic, *Kalevipoeg*, was compiled. Now the nation that had for centuries been simply 'country people' started proudly calling themselves 'Estonians'.

At the same time, key political and demographic changes were happening. Completion of the St Petersburg–Tallinn railway line in 1870 brought a wave

Inspiring words

'We shall never be great in number or strength, therefore we must become great in spirit' – pastor and linguist Jakob Hurt, a key figure in Estonia's National Awakening.

of industrial growth to Tallinn, and with it thousands of ethnic Estonian and Russian factory workers. Germans were now outnumbered in the city, and in 1904 they lost municipal elections to an Estonian-Russian bloc. For the first time, non-Germans controlled Tallinn.

A Nazi recruitment poster in 1942

THE ESTONIAN REPUBLIC

On 24 February 1918, with the imperial Russian government ousted and World War I raging, Estonia declared independence. Before the new Estonian Republic became a reality, however, it would have to undergo half a year of German occupation, then fight a 13-month War of Independence against the Bolsheviks. But by 1920, the Estonians finally had their own state.

Life in the fledgling republic was far from perfect. The economic situation remained poor through the 1920s and early '30s, and strong political divisions between right and left extremists grew ever worse. In 1934, the head of state (and later president) Konstantin Päts led a military coup d'état to keep ultra-nationalists from taking power. Though Päts stifled democracy and brought the country to near authoritarian rule, he remained a popular figure.

In the late 1930s, a long-awaited economic turnaround fuelled a building boom in Tallinn, and the republic's future looked bright.

WORLD WAR II AND OCCUPATION

World War II brought an end to the new country's aspirations. The Soviets occupied Estonia in June 1940, and immediately absorbed it into the USSR. A brutal year of arrests, executions and mass deportations to Siberian prison camps followed. Not surprisingly, when the Nazis drove out the Soviets at the end of 1941, the Estonians at first saw them as liberators. But their euphoria quickly died after it became clear that the Germans wouldn't restore independence, and when the Nazi's own harsh policies came to light. During the three-year Nazi occupation, many Estonians were co-opted into the German Army, while others joined voluntarily, seeing it as their best chance to stave off another Soviet invasion.

Anti-Soviet demonstrators in 1988

When that invasion came in September 1944, thousands of Estonians fled in boats to Sweden, establishing a strong émigré community that kept the culture alive in exile. Around 30,000–35,000 others, known as the 'Forest Brothers', hid deep in Estonia's woods and started a 10-year campaign of resistance. The worst fears about renewed Soviet atrocities came to pass. After the war, 36,000 people were arrested and accused of aiding the Nazis, and over the next years, countless families were loaded onto cattle cars and sent to Siberia.

Conditions normalised somewhat in the post-Stalin 1950s. Industries grew and hundreds of thousands of ethnic Russians were relocated to Estonia, both to work in factories, and to Russify the Soviet territory. Over the next decades, life was generally as stifled as it was in the rest of the USSR, but in many ways, the situation in Estonia was better than elsewhere – shops were better stocked and Finnish TV broadcasts provided a window to the West.

THE SINGING REVOLUTION

The seeds of Estonia's independence movement were sown during the *perestroika* years of 1987 and 1988 with the first large-scale demonstrations against the Soviet regime. Mass singing events held in June 1988, modelled on the traditional National Song Festival, saw more than 100,000 people packing Tallinn's Song Festival Grounds for several successive nights. These protests became the centre of a new national awakening and gave the movement its name, the 'Singing Revolution'.

On 20 August 1991, during a failed coup attempt in Moscow, the Supreme Soviet of the Republic of Estonia declared the nation's independence. Statues of Lenin immediately came down, and countries of the world, including the USSR, recognised Estonia's statehood. The Republic of Estonia was restored.

BOOM TIMES, SKYPE AND BEYOND

When independence was re-established, Estonia found itself facing a wrecked economy, a tense relationship with its eastern neighbour and a large, Russian-speaking minority unsure of its role in the new republic. The latter two issues came to the fore in April 2007 when the government's attempts to relocate the 'Bronze Soldier' Red Army monument from the centre of Tallinn sparked two nights of rioting by ethnic Russian youths.

For the most part, however, the latest chapter of the nation's history has been marked by healing and reintegration with the West. A brief period of 'cowboy capitalism' in the 1990s gave way to an investment and tourism boom that transformed the Tallinn skyline and boosted national pride, particularly once Estonia joined the EU in 2004. Meanwhile, tech-savvy locals in both the public and private sectors were busy building the country's reputation as a hotbed of software development, with advanced government IT services making headlines and Skype, a product created in Estonia, becoming the nation's best-known export. The term 'e-Estonia' is now widely used to describe both the country itself and this phenomenon.

The fast-paced growth of the 2005–7 period was brought to a grinding halt by the ensuing worldwide economic crisis. Estonia weathered the storm with tough, fiscal belt-tightening, eventually joining the Eurozone in 2011 – a risky but significant step in establishing itself as a player on the world stage. Recent years have been dominated by Russian aggression in Ukraine and rising border tensions, which has resulted in an increased NATO presence and the deployment of 800 British troops to Estonia in 2017.

HISTORICAL LANDMARKS

1154 Tallinn is first marked on a map by Arab cartographer al-Idrisi.

1219 King Valdemar II of Denmark conquers northern Estonia.

1227–38 Riga-based German crusaders wrest control of Tallinn and northern Estonia from the Danes; German merchants settle in Tallinn.

1248 Tallinn adopts Lübeck Law, to become a self-governing trade city.

1284 Tallinn becomes a member of the Hanseatic League.

1343–5 Estonian peasants stage the bloody St George's Night Uprising.

1346 Danes sell their Estonian holdings to the German knights in Riga, putting Estonia under the rule of the Riga-based Livonian Order.

1558–83 The Livonian War between Russia, Poland, Sweden and Denmark leaves Estonia under Swedish rule.

1684 A massive fire devastates Toompea.

1710 During the Great Northern War (1700–21), Sweden loses Estonia to the Russian Empire.

1816 Serfdom is abolished in Estonia.

1860–80 National Awakening.

1870 The St Petersburg–Tallinn rail connection is completed, sparking rapid industrial growth.

1918 Estonia declares independence, which is internationally recognised.

1940 Soviets invade, forcibly annexing Estonia into the USSR.

1941–4 Nazi invasion and occupation.

1944 Soviet forces reinvade, almost 50 years of Soviet occupation follows.

1987–8 Mass protests against Soviet rule, later to be collectively called the 'Singing Revolution'.

1991 Estonia regains independence.

2004 Estonia joins NATO and the European Union.

2011 Estonia adopts the euro.

2014 Russia allegedly abducts an Estonian border guard but returns him a year later in a spy swap

2016 Kersti Kaljulaid is elected president of Estonia

2017 800 British troops are deployed in Estonia as a deterrent to potential Russian aggression

St Nicholas Church viewed
from the Danish Garden

WHERE TO GO

When arriving in Tallinn, most visitors' first instinct is to head straight into the Old Town – and rightly so. This tightly packed ensemble of winding, cobblestone streets, beautiful medieval dwellings, breathtaking church spires, café-filled squares and half-hidden courtyards isn't just Tallinn's biggest tourist draw, it is also the heart and soul of the city. Better still, it is all neatly packaged within a centuries-old town wall, giving it a fairy-tale charm and at the same time making it easy to navigate and explore.

For a complete picture of the city, however, it is also essential to take a few steps beyond the medieval centre to see the wooden houses and offbeat attractions of Bohemian Kalamaja, the art and extravagance of Kadriorg and other surprising finds awaiting in the outlying areas.

Our tour starts at the birthplace of Tallinn – the Old Town. Today this district seems like one big, medieval mosaic, but it is actually made up of what were historically two distinct entities – Toompea Hill, home of the gentry and the representatives of Estonia's ruling power, and the Lower Town, an autonomous Hanseatic trading city populated by merchants and craftsmen.

TOOMPEA

Take one look down from the edge of this 24m (78ft) limestone hill and you will understand why Toompea has always been synonymous with power. Not only did its steep slopes provide a natural defence against would-be invaders, the high elevation gave it a commanding view of the comings and goings in the harbour nearby. It is no wonder then that ancient Estonians picked this spot to build a wooden stronghold, now thought to be the kernel

Art for sale on Pikk jalg

of Tallinn. That fortress is long gone, but the tradition it started has continued. From the Danes in 1219 to the Russians in the early 20th century, every foreign empire that ruled the northern Estonian lands has used Toompea as its power base, stationing its political representatives in Toompea Castle.

The fortified area outside the castle, meanwhile, was home to Estonia's gentry. German landlords, owners of feudal estates in the surrounding countryside, built grand, often palatial houses on Toompea from where they would look down, both literally and figuratively, on the busy merchants and workers in the Lower Town. Today most of these houses are embassies, government offices or high-priced flats.

Given Toompea's history as the seat of the ruling power, it is somehow fitting that both Estonia's Parliament and its government administration are now located here. What draws tourists to Toompea isn't these grand institutions though, it is the prospect of seeing two of the nation's most spectacular churches and getting the best views of Tallinn.

PIKK JALG AND LÜHIKE JALG

Four roads and four stairways lead up to Toompea, but by far the most interesting paths up the hill are Tallinn's two 'legs' – **Pikk jalg** ('Long Leg' Street) and **Lühike jalg** ('Short Leg' Street).

In medieval times, if you were travelling by horse or carriage, you would have taken Pikk jalg to reach Toompea from the Lower Town. It starts at the end of Pikk Street at the curious-looking **Long Leg Gate Tower** ❶ (Pika jala väravatorn) and continues in a straight, steady climb upwards to **Castle Square** (Lossi plats). The four-sided gate tower was built in 1380, but its present shape comes from a mid-15th century reconstruction. Pikk jalg itself is a favourite haunt of local artists vying to sell their works to passing tourists. High above the artists' heads, the extravagant mansions along the edge of the cliff serve as a good indication of the wealth and power of Toompea's gentry.

Picturesque Lühike jalg was historically the main pedestrian passage into Toompea. Though officially a street, this is really just a narrow, winding lane with a staircase. Today it is flanked on both sides by some of Tallinn's more intriguing art shops, and is also home to the **Adamson-Eric Museum** (https://adamson-eric. ekm.ee/en; Oct–Apr Wed–Sun 11am–6pm, May–Sep Tue–Sun), which showcases works of Adamson

Rough riding

Pikk jalg is so steep that anyone driving a carriage down it was in for a harrowing experience, according to 19th-century accounts. Before the carriage started off, coachmen and tower guards had to shout to each other to ensure that the area at the bottom was clear of traffic.

Eric (1902–68), one of the most outstanding Estonian painters and applied artists of the 20th century.

At the top of the street's 16m (52ft) climb stands the **Short Leg Gate Tower ❷** (Lühikese jala väravatorn), built in 1456. The sturdy, wooden door you pass here is original and dates from the 17th century.

ORTHODOX CATHEDRAL

When you reach Castle Square at the top of Toompea, you come to a dramatic, onion-domed church that looks like something straight out of a Russian novel. This is the **Aleksander Nevsky Cathedral ❸** (Sun–Fri 8am–7pm, Sat 8am–8pm; free), the most impressive-looking Orthodox church in Estonia and an important place of worship for Tallinn's Orthodox faithful. Built from 1894 to 1900, the cathedral is a relatively new addition to Toompea. It was designed by St Petersburg architect Mikhail Preobrazhensky and follows the same basic layout as the five-domed churches that started to appear in Moscow and Jaroslavl in the 17th century.

Though the cathedral serves a purely spiritual purpose these days, it was originally placed here as a blatant symbol of Russian power. In the late 19th century, imperial Russia was carrying out an intense campaign of Russification in its outer provinces. As part of its drive to assert cultural dominance over the mainly Lutheran Germans and Estonians, the tsarist government built this towering Orthodox cathedral directly in front of the castle, right on what had been one of the city's most famous squares.

A chance to look at the cathedral's interior shouldn't be passed up. Visitors are welcome to come in and view the abundance of awe-inspiring **icons**, mosaics and other works of religious art that line the walls. The cathedral also operates a small gift shop to the right of the entrance.

TOOMPEA CASTLE

Next to the cathedral stands a large pink edifice that bears a distinctly regal look. This is the front of **Toompea Castle** ❹ (Toompea Loss), historic seat of power in Estonia and home to the Riigikogu Estonia's parliament. The castle's origins go back to 1227–9, when the Knights of the Sword replaced the wooden stronghold that pagan Estonians had used to defend the hill with their

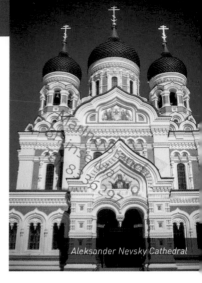

Aleksander Nevsky Cathedral

own square fortress, which they surrounded with a circular, stone wall. In the 14th century this was rebuilt into a convent-style fortress with a trapezoidal inner courtyard, 20m (65ft) high walls, and four corner towers, three of which are still standing. The **baroque palace** you see in front of you was built from 1767 to 73 on the order of Russian Empress Catherine the Great, and served as the administration building for the Russian provincial government in Estonia during tsarist times. The three-storey **Parliament Building** (www.riigikogu.ee; Mon–Fri 10am–4pm, booking ahead and valid photo identification document are essential; guided tour in English Fri at 11am; free) in the courtyard, not visible from the outside, was built in 1920–2 on the foundations of the former convent and reflects an Expressionist style.

The **Governor's Garden** to the left of the castle is the best place to view another Tallinn landmark, **Tall Hermann** (Pikk Hermann) tower. The tower was built onto the corner of the

Tall Hermann tower and the Parliament
Building at Governor's Gardens

castle in 1371, but only reached its final 46m (150ft) height
after reconstruction in 1500. Tradition dictates that which-
ever nation flies its flag on Tall Hermann rules Estonia. On
24 February 1989, in what was one of the boldest gestures of
Estonia's push for independence from the USSR, the Estonian
blue, black and white flag was raised here in place of the red
Soviet one. Estonia's colours have flown on Tall Hermann every
day since – a potent symbol of the nation's sovereignty.

To see the castle's most medieval-looking side, take a quick
detour down Falgi Street, south of the fortress, and then return
to Toompea to see more of the town's old defences.

KIEK IN DE KÖK AND BASTION TUNNELS

Take the steps leading down from the south side of Aleksander
Nevsky Cathedral and continue through a small park. Here
you'll see a large, round medieval tower that looks like it could

stand up to any amount of cannon fire. This is **Kiek in de Kõk** ❺, the Baltic region's most powerful cannon tower. Its name, which in Low German literally means 'peek into the kitchen', refers to the tower's 36m (118ft) height. Soldiers posted here joked that they could see right down the chimneys and into the kitchens of the houses below.

Kiek in de Kõk was built in 1475–6 as a much smaller tower, and then almost immediately rebuilt to give it its current mammoth size. It was finally put to the test during the Livonian War (1558–83) when Ivan the Terrible's forces besieged Tallinn twice, once blowing a hole in its top floor massive enough 'to drive two oxen through', according to historic accounts.

Now the tower operates as an extensive, modern **museum** (http://linnamuuseum.ee/en/kiek-de-kok; Tue–Sun

⊙ KALEV'S GRAVE

According to legend, Toompea is actually the burial mound of Kalev, the mythical figure who founded Tallinn. When Kalev died, his grief-stricken widow Linda started to cover his grave with stone after stone, and the poor woman kept at it until she had created this bulging hill.

During the construction of the Aleksander Nevsky Cathedral, a rumour surfaced that workers digging the space for the foundations had stumbled onto Kalev's grave. They supposedly uncovered an iron door bearing the inscription 'Cursed be anyone who dares disturb my peace'. As building continued, cracks started to appear in the cathedral's foundations. People took this as a sign of impending doom either for the cathedral or for Tallinn as a whole. Luckily, the much-feared disaster never came to pass.

Kiek in de Kök

10am–5.30pm) chronicling the development of the town and its defences from the 13th to the 18th century. Apart from seeing the weaponry and other displays, a visit here will allow you to climb the old staircases that run through the tower's 4m (13ft) thick walls and enjoy the dizzying view from the top floor.

The museum is also the gateway to the **Bastion Tunnels**, the once-secret defence system that runs under this edge of Toompea. Originally built in the late 1600s to ferry powder and soldiers, the tunnels found new life in the 20th century as a bomb shelter. Visiting requires signing up for a group tour in advance. Enquire at the ticket desk or phone ahead (tel: 644 6686). The tour includes an informational film and may include a 'train ride' towards the Swedish bastion or a visit to the Carved Sone Museum.

DANISH KING'S GARDEN

On the way back to Castle Square you can get a good look at more towers by following the thick town wall on the right. Crossing through a rectangular passage in the wall near the church takes you to the **Danish King's Garden ❻** (Taani kuninga aed), an open area at the top of Lühike jalg, from where a set of terraced steps leads down to Rüütli Street. According to legend, this is the birthplace of the Danish flag. King Valdemar

II supposedly camped on this spot when his forces were first trying to conquer Toompea in 1219. The Danes were losing the battle when suddenly the skies opened up and a red flag with a white cross floated downwards from the heavens. Spurred on by this miraculous sign, the Danes were able to fight on to victory.

The two towers here, the small, round **Stable Tower** (Tallitorn) and the larger, square **Maiden's Tower** (Neitsitorn), both date from the 14th century. The name 'Maiden's Tower' is an exercise in medieval irony   the tower was actually a prison for prostitutes.

DOME CHURCH

Both Toom-Kooli Street and Piiskopi Street lead from Castle Square to **Church Square** (Kiriku plats), home to the majestic-looking **Dome Church** ❼ (Toomkirik; http://toomkirik.ee), which is the headquarters of the Lutheran church of Estonia. Officially called the **Cathedral of St Mary the Virgin**, the Dome Church was probably established not long after the Danes arrived in Toompea in 1219. Records first mention the church in 1233, by which time Dominican monks had already replaced the original wooden structure with one constructed of stone. The church's vaulted main body is thought to originate from a 14th-century rebuilding.

In 1684 a devastating fire ripped through Toompea destroying nearly every building, including the Dome Church. Though the church was operating again two years later, reconstruction work took until the end of the century. The **baroque tower**, open to visitors in summer, was a later addition; it dates from 1778–9.

The most striking aspect of the church's interior is the huge collection of funereal **coats of arms** covering the walls. These intricate works of art, dating mostly from the 17th to the 20th century, traditionally accompanied the casket during funeral processions, and were later kept in the church as a memorial.

The Dome Church

Most reflect a baroque style, as does the rest of the church's interior. The intricate **baroque pulpit** and **high altar** were both carved by the Tallinn sculptor Christian Ackermann and completed in 1696.

Along the northern wall, opposite the entrance, are the lavish **tombs** of some fairly eminent historic figures. These include Pontus de la Gardie (died 1585), French-born head of Swedish forces during the Livonian War; A.J. von Krusenstern (died 1848), a Baltic German explorer who was the first to circumnavigate the globe under the Russian flag; and Admiral Samuel Greig of Fife, Scotland (1735–88), commander of Russia's Baltic Fleet and reputed lover of Catherine the Great.

VIEWING PLATFORMS

Heading from the church down Kohtu Street will take you past some impressive 18th- and 19th-century houses once owned by Toompea's noble elite. The street soon ends at the **Kohtu Street viewing platform** ❽. From here there is a truly spectacular view of the red-tiled roofs of the medieval Lower Town as well as the modern-looking city beyond the town walls.

The roof in the immediate foreground with the cockerel-shaped weathervane belongs to the Long Leg Gate Tower, its fairy-tale look contrasting sharply with the contemporary skyline. The tall, medieval church on the left towards the port is St Olav's Church; the one much closer and on the right is St Nicholas's Church. Among the buildings in the centre of the Lower Town, you can make out the two very similar towers of the Town Hall and the Holy Spirit Church.

Further in the distance, beyond the high-rise hotels and office blocks, you can make out the arched rim of the **Tallinn Song Festival Arena** and the triangle-shaped ruins of **St Bridget's Convent**. The spire on the horizon is Tallinn's **TV Tower**, and the rows of giant apartment blocks to its right mark the suburb of Lasnamäe.

A slightly different view is on offer at the nearby **Patkuli viewing platform** ❾, which can be reached by turning right on Toom-Rüütli, then left at the end of that street onto a nearly hidden passage. This platform looks over the northern section of the Lower Town and affords an excellent view, taking in St Olav's Church, the **town wall** and several of its **towers**.

The lavish manor house standing on the cliff immediately to the left of the platform is **Stenbock House** ❿ (Stenbocki maja; www.riigi kantselei.ee/stenbock/eng. html). Built in the late 18th century, it has been a courthouse and, at one time, a private home. After years of Soviet-era dilapidation it was restored in the 1990s and is now the office of the Government of Estonia.

A step down

After Toompea burned in 1684, there was so much rubble in the area that the ground level was raised by more than a metre. Because workers used the original floor when rebuilding Dome Church, anyone now entering the church has to take several steps down from street level.

Tallinn's characteristic towers

From the Patkuli viewing platform you can head straight down Rahukohtu Street to continue touring Toompea, or make your way down the Patkuli Steps and into the Lower Town.

LOWER TOWN

For most visitors, it is Lower Town (All-Linn) that defines Tallinn. This is where the crowds mingle, where bicycle taxis, Segway riders and costumed almond sellers jostle for space on the medieval streets, where tourists come to gaze at historic curiosities of every sort or simply to relax and take in the timeless atmosphere of the Old Town. In short, this is where life happens in Tallinn.

In that respect, little has changed since medieval times. The area we now call the Lower Town was then the Hanseatic city of Tallinn (or Reval, as it was known at the time), a busy trading city of international stature. In 1248 it was granted autonomous status and from then on had its own government, local laws, social institutions and defence forces. More importantly, it was the domain of merchants and artisans, labourers and servants, all of whom would have contributed to the general bustle of commerce as they went about their daily routines.

Centuries of activity have left the Lower Town with a wealth of fascinating sights, many of which are nicely complemented by the museums, cafés and other businesses operating among them.

TOWN HALL SQUARE

Through the centuries, the social and cultural heart of Tallinn has always been **Town Hall Square** ⑪ (Raekoja plats), the attractive open area at the centre of the Old Town. In medieval times it served as the town's main marketplace and was also the site of tournaments, festivals and at least one execution. Even now the square acts as the chief gathering place for the city's residents, each year hosting scores of concerts, art markets and festival events. Town Hall Square is invariably packed with umbrella-shaded café terraces in spring and summer, and every winter it is home to an elaborate Christmas market

⊙ THE TOWN WALL

Stone barricades had been established around Tallinn as early as 1265, but the town wall's current shape comes from an extensive reconstruction undertaken in the 14th century. The wall was continually improved through the years and, by its heyday in the 16th century, it was 2.4km (1.5 miles) long, 14–16m (46–52ft) high, up to 3m (10ft) thick, and had a total of 46 towers. Today 1.9km (1.2 miles) of the wall are still standing, as are 20 defence towers, two inner gate towers, and sections of two outer gate towers.

The closest segment of the wall you see from the Patkuli viewing platform, connecting **Nunna**, **Sauna** and **Kuldjala** towers, is open to tourists. A visit here is the best way to see Tallinn's defences up close and to enjoy wonderful views of Toompea. When in the Lower Town, follow your map to the corner of Gümnaasiumi and Suur-Kloostri, and look for the entrance to the **Town Wall** (Linnamüür; June–Aug daily 11am–7pm, Apr–May and Sept–Oct Fri–Wed 11am–5pm, Nov–Mar Fri–Sun 11am–4pm).

at the centre of which stands the town Christmas tree, a tradition dating back to at least 1441.

Presiding over the square is Tallinn's **Town Hall** (Raekoda; http://raekoda.tallinn.ee; July–Aug Mon–Sat 10am–4pm). Historic records indicate that another town hall occupied this spot as early as 1322, but the late-Gothic structure you see today was completed in 1404. **Old Thomas** (Vana Toomas), the soldier-shaped weathervane perched atop the spire, has been watching over the city since 1530, while the baroque spire itself and the fanciful, dragon-shaped drainpipes both date from 1627.

Tallinn's powerful Town Council would hold meetings on the hall's main floor upstairs, where the beautiful, vaulted **Citizens' Hall** and **Council Chamber** are located. The wooden benches that occupy them are decorated with intricate, medieval carvings

Cafés and market stalls in the attractive Town Hall Square

that easily qualify as art treasures. The ground floor, by contrast, was more a place of business, encompassing a trading hall, treasury and counting room, while the building's basement housed a torture chamber. Unfortunately, the Town Hall is open to drop-in visitors only during July and August, but visits can be arranged for all other times of the year by appointment (tel: 6457 900). Anyone not afraid of heights should also climb the 64m (210ft) **Town Hall Tower** (Raekoja torn; May–15 Sept daily 11am–6pm) for a great view of the Old Town.

Tucked behind the Town Hall is the 15th-century **Town Hall Prison** (Raevangla) where those arrested were kept before trial. It now houses an interesting **Museum of Photography** (www.linnamuuseum.ee/fotomuuseum; Wed–Mon 10.30am–6pm) chronicling 150 years of Tallinn's photographic pursuits and displaying numerous antique cameras. Some exhibits occupy the old cells, downstairs.

Back on Town Hall Square you'll see thousands of stones covering the ground, but there is one of particular interest – a large, round slab decorated with a compass rose. You can find it by standing at the corner of the Town Hall, directly in front of the café, and following a seam in the pattern of bricks 25 or 30 paces out into the square. Tour guides call this stone the **Centre of Tallinn**, a name that isn't based so much on geography as it is on the fact that you can theoretically see the tops of all five

An outdoor café on Town Hall Square

of the Old Town's spires from here. Be prepared to stretch, bend and/or jump to achieve this goal.

In a corner of the square opposite the Town Hall stands the **Town Hall Pharmacy** (Raeapteek), one of the oldest, continuously running pharmacies in Europe. Records first mention it in 1422, but it may have been established decades earlier. Amazingly, from 1580 to 1911 the pharmacy was managed by 10 generations of the same family. Some of the useful preparations sold here in centuries past include minced bat, burnt bees, snakeskin and powdered unicorn horn. Everyday items such as paper, wax, gunpowder and claret were available as well. A dubious local legend even insists that marzipan was invented here.

These days you'll find the same remedies here as in any modern pharmacy, but in homage to its history, the location maintains a small **exhibition room** (www.raeapteek.ee; Mon–Sat 10am–6pm; free) displaying antique pharmacy equipment, archaic medicines and similar artefacts.

HOLY SPIRIT CHURCH

Just a few paces north of Town Hall Square through Saiakang passage stands a radiant, white church with an octagonal tower. This is the **Holy Spirit Church** ⑫ (Püha Vaimu kirik; Mon–Fri 10am–3pm, Sat 10am–4pm, Sun between services), tiny in comparison to the Old Town's other medieval churches, but enormous in the hearts of ordinary Estonians for the role it played in their cultural history. It was here that the very first sermons were given in the Estonian language after the Reformation, and in 1535 the church's pastor, Johann Koell, translated and published what is thought to be the first book in Estonian. Balthasar Russow, one of the most important chroniclers of the

CRIME AND PUNISHMENT

In addition to the other functions it had in medieval times, Town Hall Square served as a place of public punishment. For example, women accused of gossiping were sentenced to walk around the square three times while enduring the whistling and jeering of the crowds. Look for the iron shackles that are mounted on one pillar of the Town Hall. These were used to punish people guilty of petty crimes such as swindling and non-payment of debts. In more serious cases, convicts would be locked in a pillory that once stood on the square.

The town also employed an executioner, but as a rule the executions took place on a hill outside the town. One notable exception occurred in the late 17th century. A drunken priest named Panicke ordered an omelette at an inn, and finding it 'hard as the sole of a shoe', sent it back. Upon being served two more such horrendous omelettes, he grabbed an axe and slaughtered the waitress. Once sober, the priest turned himself in, begging to be executed. So heinous was his crime that the sentence was carried out immediately, right on the square. Two long stones in the shape of an 'L', not far from the Town Hall Pharmacy, mark the place where he was beheaded, though the spot may be covered by café tables in summer.

A colourful town house beside the Church of the Holy Spirit

Livonian period, was pastor here from 1566 until his death in 1600.

The church was important to Tallinn's medieval administration as well: it served as a chapel for the Town Council, and one of its rooms was used for signing contracts and treaties, the sanctity of the church ensuring the subsequent honesty of all parties. Mostly, however, this was a church for the common folk. As early as the 13th century it operated an almshouse tending to the city's sick, elderly and poor, and in contrast to other churches, the Holy Spirit Church's congregation was made up of Tallinn's lower class.

The building was completed in the 1360s and its overall shape dates from that period. Its **baroque spire**, however, is a newer installation; it was added after a major fire in 1684 destroyed its Renaissance-style predecessor. The most eye-catching addition to the church is the large, blue-and-gold **clock** on the exterior of the building near the main door-way. Created by Tallinn's best-known woodcarver, Christian Ackermann, in the late 17th-century, this is the city's oldest – and by far its most captivating – public timepiece. The figures you see in each of its corners represent the four gospels.

As attractive as both the spire and clock are, the church's most impressive feature is unquestionably its rich interior. Decorated from almost floor to ceiling with lavishly carved woodwork, including baroque pews and a Renaissance pulpit, the ensemble is truly awe-inspiring. The church's best-loved piece is the **altar**, commissioned from the renowned Lübeck sculptor and painter Bernt Notke in 1483. Figures of the Virgin Mary with child, apostles and saints, all painted in bright, clear blue, red and gold, stand at the centre of the cupboard-type altarpiece.

THE GUILDS OF PIKK STREET

Leading from the area just north of Town Hall Square to the northernmost tip of the Old Town is the aptly named Pikk Street, or 'Long Street'. It was the longest street in medieval Tallinn, a busy artery connecting the port to the town's main

⊘ THE CAT'S WELL

Tallinn was not always the most animal-friendly place in times past. On the corner of Rataskaevu and Dunkri streets stands a picturesque, covered wheel well, the subject of countless tourist snapshots. Few visitors who pass by here realise that the well has a highly unsavoury legend attached to it.

In medieval times, local residents believed that a water spirit lived in the well, and that it would become angry and flood the town unless they gave it regular animal sacrifices. So all sorts of animals – mostly dead but some living – were thrown down the well. The main victims of this superstitious practice were stray neighbourhood cats, giving rise to the well's popular nickname, 'Cat's Well'.

The practice did little to improve the quality of the water drawn from here, though in reality, the problem may have had more to do with a high lime content. In either case, the well fell into disuse by the 19th century and was filled in.

marketplace. Not only was it the principal route for merchants visiting Tallinn, it was also home to several guild associations.

From the 14th century, guilds, all-important associations of merchants and craftsmen, played a major role in town politics and society. Though many guilds took on the character of religious brotherhoods, they were actually profession-based organisations that acted as both trade unions and the architects of Tallinn's social life, organising weddings, feasts and public celebrations.

The grand looking building at Pikk 17, just across from the Holy Spirit Church, is the **Great Guild Hall** ⑬ (Suurgildi hoone), which served as a meeting place for Tallinn's Great Guild, a group of wealthy merchants that wielded considerable influence over town affairs. The hall was completed around 1410 and has changed little since that time. The red and white symbols on its facade represent the guild's coat of arms, and the fanciful, lion's-head doorknockers date from 1430. The hall is now home to the **Estonian History Museum** (www.ajaloomuuseum.ee; May–Sep daily 10am–6pm, Oct–Apr Tue–Sun 10am–6pm), which presents a high-tech, engaging overview of 11,000 years of the nation's development. The exhibition in the cellar provides insight into the building itself and how it was used through the years, while

Sweet tooth café

The city's oldest café, **Maiasmokk** (Sweet tooth; www.kohvikmaiasmokk.ee/en), has been selling cakes and pastries from the same spot at Pikk 16 since 1864. Guests can sip coffee while basking in its early 20th-century ambience. A separate entrance around the corner leads into the **Kalev Marzipan Museum Room** (www.kalev.eu; daily 10am–7pm; free), where hundreds of elaborate marzipan figurines are on display.

Keeping time at the Holy Spirit Church

paving slabs in Börsi kaik lane outside each have a historic event marked on them, forming a timeline of Estonia's past (with a few references to its possible future).

Further north along Pikk, on the right-hand side, you'll see the eccentric facade of the **Dragon Gallery**, (www.eaa.ee/draakon), with its carved seahorse-tailed serpents and Egyptian slaves. Created by Tartu-born Jacques Rosenbaum in 1910, this is by far the most memorable art nouveau facade in Tallinn.

The bright, triple-gabled **Kanut Guild Hall** (Kanuti gildi hoone) stands next door to it at Pikk 20. This was home to the Kanut Guild, which united skilled craftsmen from a number of different trades. The house's present, Tudor-style appearance comes from an 1860s remodelling, its overall look inspired by English Gothic architecture. The two bold-looking statues on its facade represent St Kanut and Martin Luther. The house is now used as a dance theatre (www.saal.ee).

Brotherhood of Black Heads doorway

High up, across the street from the Kanut Guild Hall, is the somewhat bizarre figure of a monocle-wearing man gazing down. There are several theories as to why he was put here; the most amusing is that a jealous wife installed it to break her husband's habit of spying on the ladies as they practised ballet in the upper floors of the guild hall.

At Pikk 26 you come to the eye-catching **House of the Brotherhood of Black Heads** ⑭ (Mustpeade Maja; www.mustpeademaja.ee; guided tours available). The brotherhood, a guild of young, unmarried merchants, played a major role in medieval Tallinn's life and politics, organising the town's defence and, among other duties, arranging annual tournaments and celebrations. The guild's curious name comes from the fact that its patron saint, St Mauritius, was a dark-skinned Moor. The exquisite Renaissance facade dates from 1597, and its beautiful, carved wooden door, one of the most recognised architectural elements in Tallinn, was installed in 1640. The house is now used as a concert hall, but in summer, when no events are scheduled, visitors can drop in to look at its gorgeous, vaulted White Hall and Olav's Hall, as well as an intriguing, indoor courtyard.

Further down the street, a careful observer will notice something eerie about the building at Pikk 59. Its cellar windows are completely bricked over – a detail that gives it a decidedly ominous appearance. This was the **KGB Headquarters** during the Soviet period. In this sad place many people were tortured and shot; others were interrogated before being sent to Siberia. A placard sat on the front of the building which read, 'Here stands the headquarters of the organ of repression of the Soviet Occupation – the road of suffering for Estonians.' After being inaccessible for many years, the prison cells are now open (www.okupatsioon.ee; Mon–Fri 10am–6pm, Oct–Apr from 11am; guided tours available, booking in advance required).

ST OLAV'S CHURCH

Just a few paces further on is Tallinn's largest medieval structure, the enormous **St Olav's Church** ⓯ (Oleviste kirik). A short walk around its side, towards Lai Street, will give you a better view of its sheer magnitude. The church was first mentioned in historic records in 1267, and originally served a Scandinavian merchants' camp that occupied this end of Pikk Street in the 13th century. The basic shape it has today, however, comes from rebuilding undertaken in the 15th century.

In 1500, an absurdly tall (159m/522ft), Gothic-style pavilion steeple was built onto the top of the tower, making St Olav's Church the tallest building in the world in 1549, when the spire of England's Lincoln Cathedral collapsed. The hope was that the huge steeple would act as a helpful signpost for ships approaching the busy, commercial town. The steeple indeed proved to be a useful advertising tool, but it turned out to be even better as a lightning rod. Numerous bolts struck the steeple through

Calling all spies

During Soviet times, the neighbouring KGB office used St Olav's metal spire as an antenna for its radio communications.

the centuries, and twice, once in 1625 and again in 1820, the church was burned to the ground. The steeple you now see was installed after the first fire, and is only 124m (407ft) tall. From April to October, energetic visitors can make the arduous climb to the top of the **church tower** (daily July–Aug 10am–8pm, Apr–June and Sept–Oct 10am–6pm) for spectacular views of Toompea and the Old Town.

THE GREAT COAST GATE AND VICINITY

Humbler in size than the church but just as awe-inspiring is **The Three Sisters** ⑯ (Kolm õde), at Pikk 71, a magnificently restored ensemble made up of three brightly painted, 15th-century ter-raced houses attached in a sibling-like way. The houses and their beautiful facades – including an intricate, baroque front door

⊙ SOVIET INSIGHTS

Signs of the nation's Soviet past, some subtle, others blatant, are everywhere in Tallinn, but visitors with a particular interest in this chapter of the nation's history should keep a couple of opportunities in mind. The Museum of Occupations at Toom-pea 8 (www.okupatsioon.ee; closed for renovation) provides a high-tech and dramatic introduction to the 1940–91 period. The more humorous aspects of Soviet life come out on a tour of the Viru Hotel and its KGB Museum. The hotel was the official stopping place for foreign guests to the city and as such was rife with intrigue. Its upper floor also housed a secret radio room. The museum can only be visited by tour, but it is well worth the trouble for the hilarious stories and insights into everyday Soviet life it dishes out. Enquire at the hotel reception (www.sokoshotels.fi) or phone ahead (tel: 680 9300).

The Three Sisters

from 1651 – are striking examples of medieval architecture. The Three Sisters now operate as a luxury hotel (www.3s.ee).

The street ends at the **Great Coast Gate ⑰** (Suur Rannavärav). This and the Viru Gates on Viru Street are all that remain of the six powerful, medieval gates that once regulated access to Tallinn. The Great Coast Gate – actually a collection of towers and gates – was founded in the early 1300s, but its largest and most famous piece, **Fat Margaret's Tower** (Paks Margareeta), was built from 1511 to 1530. The squat, round cannon tower can best be seen from outside the gate. With a diameter of 25m (82ft) and walls that were up to 5m (17ft) thick, the tower was a formidable part of the town's defences.

The tower now houses the **Estonian Maritime Museum** (Eesti Meremuuseum; www.meremuuseum.ee; closed for renovation until summer 2019); another branch of the museum is at the Seaplane Harbour (see page 59), with four floors of displays presenting the nation's seafaring history from Neolithic times to the present, and views of the town and harbour from the roof. On the grassy hill outside the tower you'll see a row of medieval cannons, and a large monument in the shape of an incomplete bridge. The latter is a memorial to the victims of the *Estonia* ferry disaster. The 15,000-tonne ferry sank en route from Tallinn to Stockholm on 28 September 1994, resulting in 852 fatalities.

From here, wooden steps lead down to Uus Street, from where you can reach Vene Street and the Latin Quarter.

THE LATIN QUARTER

The area at the end of Vene Street has come to be called Tallinn's 'Latin Quarter' thanks to the presence of a Dominican Monastery that operated here from the 13th to the 16th century. The monastery itself, or what remains of it, still defines the area, but these days a number of newer sights add to the fascinating milieu of this corner of the Old Town.

One example can be found at the end of Vene Street in the form of the impressive **St Nicholas's Orthodox Church** (Püha Nikolai Imetegija kirik). This neoclassical, Russian Orthodox church, with its copper dome and double towers, was built in the 1820s by St Petersburg-based Swiss architect Luigi Rusca. Visitors shouldn't be afraid to look inside at the iconostasis, said to rival the most beautiful in Estonia. Across the street from the church, at Vene 17, a well-restored medieval house is home to the **Tallinn City Museum** (Tallinna Linnamuuseum; www.linnamuuseum.ee; Tue–Mon Mar–Oct 10.30am–6pm; Nov–Feb 10am–5.30pm). Well worth a visit, this extensive, modern museum chronicles the city's development from its founding right up to post-Soviet times.

Vene Street's main feature is the **Dominican Monastery** ⑱ (Dominiklaste Klooster). Known as St Catherine's Monastery, it was founded here in 1246 by the Dominican Order and, until the

Reformation, played a key role in the town's religious affairs. The monastery wasn't always popular with Tallinn's ruling elite, however, because the monks' work was often too supportive of the common Estonian people. The monastery was closed down after the Reformation in 1525, and in 1531 the abandoned complex was ravaged by fire.

Fat Margaret's Tower

Now all that remains of the monastery are the **courtyard** and a few of its surrounding hallways and chambers. In summer you can stroll along St Catherine's Passage (see below) to Müürivahe 33, site of the **Dominican Monastery Claustrum** (www.claustrum.eu; 15 May–30 Sept daily 11am–5pm). This institution gives access to the monastery's inner chambers, such as the prior's living quarters, monks' dormitory, library and refectory. The mysterious '**energy pillar**' in the cellar is believed to give off a kind of psychic force.

Tallinn's most picturesque lane, **St Catherine's Passage** (Katariina käik), connects Vene and Müürivahe streets just south of the monastery. A long row of 15th–17th-century structures on one side of the passage houses **St Catherine's Guild** (Katariina gild; www.katariinagild.eu), where a group of women artists use traditional methods to create modern-looking and sometimes offbeat handicrafts. Visitors can drop in and watch them working away on quilts, ceramics, glass, silk designs, jewellery and fine leatherwork. The opposite side

Dance of Death by Bernt Notke in St Nicholas's Orthodox Church

of the passage displays some intriguing – if somewhat eerie – stone burial slabs that were removed from the St Catherine's Church directly behind them.

ST NICHOLAS'S CHURCH

St Nicholas's Church ⑲ (Niguliste kirik), which looks proudly over Harju Street, was the only church in the Lower Town not to be ransacked during the Reformation of 1524, thanks to its head of congregation, who successfully kept the mobs out by pouring molten lead into the locks. Dedicated to the patron saint of merchants and artisans, it was founded by a group of German settlers who had set up a trading yard here in the early 13th century. Because it was built before Tallinn's town wall was completed, the church was outfitted with heavy wooden beams to bar the doors and hiding places for those escaping attack. The main body and choir were modernised in the 15th century, though the appearance the church has now is the result of constant rebuilding since then. The church was destroyed in the Soviet bombing raid of March 1944 (see box), and was painstakingly reconstructed from 1956 to 1984.

St Nicholas's now serves a purely secular function, operating as the **Niguliste Museum and Concert Hall** (https://niguliste muuseum.ekm.ee/en; Wed–Sun 10am–5pm, May–Sep Tue–Sun), which showcases religious art from Estonia and abroad. Art lovers should definitely not pass up an opportunity to visit this fascinating church-turned-museum. It has the distinction of containing Estonia's most famous work of art, 15th-century

⊙ WORLD WAR II DESTRUCTION

Sharp-eyed travellers will notice that the side of Harju Street near St Nicholas's Church is strangely devoid of buildings. This absence is a sad testament to the night of 9 March 1944, when approximately 300 Soviet Army planes bombed Tallinn, killing more than 550 civilians, destroying entire neighbourhoods and leaving 20 percent of the population homeless. Locals often point out that, of the 3,068 bombs dropped, not a single one hit a military target. The area of Old Town hardest hit was Harju Street, where this entire block was reduced to rubble and remained mostly turfed over for the ensuing decades.

In 2007, as the city was redeveloping the area into a park and ice rink, it created a memorial to the bombing by unearthing and restoring Trepi tänav (Stairway Street), a lane that once ran between two buildings between Harju and the church. At its top is Needle-Eye Gate, partly reconstructed from its original pieces, which had been stored away in museums. Glass openings at the base of the street provide a glimpse into the cellars of the houses that once stood here.

artist Bernt Notke's mural **_Dance Macabre_** (Dance with Death), a frightening masterpiece depicting people from various walks of life dancing with skeletons. Other treasures in the museum include awe-inspiring altars from the 16th and 17th centuries, a collection of Renaissance and baroque chandeliers, and several curious 14th–17th-century tombstones. The museum also houses a **Silver Chamber** displaying exquisite ceremonial items from Tallinn's guilds. Making use of its wonderful acoustics, the church hosts **organ concerts** on weekend afternoons. A concert schedule is posted outside.

FREEDOM SQUARE

Freedom Square 20 (Vabaduse väljak), at the southern tip of the Old Town, is central Tallinn's 'other' main square. In striking contrast to its rival, Town Hall Square, it has a decidedly modern look. It was rescued from its decades-long parking-lot status in 2009 when, after an extensive makeover, it was given back to the townspeople.

One of the additions during the makeover was the towering **War of Independence Victory Column** that dominates the square's western edge. Topped by a likeness of the Cross of Liberty medal, the glass-plated column is the centrepiece of a memorial to the country's 1918–20 struggle against Germany and Soviet Russia.

A look around the square will reveal multiple layers of the city's history: a glass viewing area at the Harju Street corner lets passers-by peer down at the underground remnants of the medieval Harju Gate; the late-19th-century **St John's Church** (Jaani kirik) presides over the square's east side; and most other buildings visible here, including the hotel, Russian Drama Theatre and city offices across Karli Boulevard, reflect a definite 1930s style – a result of the pre-war economic boom.

PARKS AND MOATS

Mysteriously overlooked by most visitors, the scenic parks and paths that ring the east side of the Old Town offer a picture-perfect view of the town fortifications, not to mention a relaxing escape from the tourist crowds. The large, green area that starts at Freedom Square and extends nearly to Fat Margaret's Tower was once part of a system of bastions and moats that protected the town from attack. Now it is a favourite place for Tallinners of all ages to stroll.

Starting from Freedom Square you can ascend the stone steps next to the victory column and then the paths to the peak of **Harju Hill** (Harjumägi) for views of the surrounding city. Working your way west past the Kiek in de Kök tower, you soon reach Toompea Street, from where you can either descend to the lower **Hirve Park**, or continue along Falgi Street to the next rise, **Linda Hill** (Lindamägi). At its top stands a solemn **monument ㉑** to the mythical figure Linda, whose husband Kalev, according to ancient lore, founded the town (see page 33). The statue predates World War II, but what's significant about it is that Tallinn residents adopted it during Soviet times as a kind

Linda Hill monument

Schnelli Pond in Toompark with the 18th-century Stenbock House behind

of unsanctioned memorial to loved ones deported to Siberia. Since there would be no gravesite and no official memorial, relatives would lay flowers here, at considerable risk to themselves if they were caught. Even now the tradition continues, and a plaque that has been added reads, 'To remember the ones who were taken away'.

From Linda Hill, cross Falgi and take the stairs downwards. From here, the view becomes more scenic with Toompea Castle and the sharp cliffs below coming into sight. A jog to the left around the football pitch brings you to **Toompark** ㉒, whose paths and bridges surround **Schnelli Pond** (Schnelli tiik), the only remaining part of the town's water-filled moat. Finally, a walk through the **Square of Towers** ㉓ (Tornide väljak), another green area just north of Nunne Street, offers the best possible view of Tallinn's medieval wall and towers. In spring and summer, this is the site of the city's International

Flower Festival, where you can tour elaborate and often outlandish gardening arrangements. From here, a break in the wall will take you back into the Lower Town.

KALAMAJA

With its colourful wooden houses, offbeat galleries and popular cafés, the up-and-coming Kalamaja neighbourhood, just outside Old Town, presents the edgier side of the city's character, as well as some must-see sights. The part-residential part-industrial area grew up in the late 19th and early 20th centuries, when the coming of the railway sparked an influx of factories and workers. Thanks to this phenomenon, a quaint and curious hotchpotch of homes, in varying states of repair, now lines most of Kalamaja's quiet streets.

Start at the railway station, taking in the architecture along Vabriku, Valgevase and Töötuse streets, before making your way along Vana-Kalamaja towards the bay. The street ends at a staircase leading towards the ominous **Patarei Prison** ㉔ (Patarei Vangla). Originally built as a sea fortress in the early 19th century, it served as a prison and execution site through the Soviet era and was finally closed in 2002. Most of the sprawling territory has been left as it was, though some buildings now house art galleries, and a seaside café operates here in summer. The **Prison Museum** (Vanglamuuseum; www.patarei.org) is now closed, but is still offering themed tours of other parts of Tallinn.

Adjacent to the prison to the west is Kalamaja's biggest attraction, the **Seaplane Harbour** ㉓ (Lennusadam; www.lennusadam.eu; May–Sept daily 10am–7pm, Oct–Apr Tue–Sun 10am–6pm), a branch of the Estonian Maritime Museum (see page 51). Opened in 2012, this museum and activity centre makes its home in and around a set of domed seaplane hangars dating to the World War I era. The vast interior displays boats, mines and anti-aircraft guns, while hands-on exhibits let visitors attempt to shoot down helicopters, make paper aeroplanes and try on old military uniforms. Pride of place in the hall is given to the ***Lembit* submarine**, built in Barrow-in-Furness, England, in 1936 for the Estonian Navy and later co-opted into the Soviet fleet. Visitors can climb inside to inspect the torpedo hatches, crew's bunks and the like.

The outdoor exhibit comprises a handful of ships that can be toured, including the ***Suur Tõll* icebreaker**, built in 1914, the largest intact steam-powered icebreaker in the world.

From the harbour and prison area, a paved pathway called the 'Cultural Kilometer' follows the shoreline east towards the Passenger Harbour, ending at the Culture Cauldron, an art centre housed in a former heating plant. The **Estonian Museum of Contemporary Art** (EKKM; www.ekkm.ee; Apr–Dec Tue–Sun noon–7pm; free) that makes its home here shows off the generation's latest creations. Students of architecture might also want to climb the nearby **Linnahall ㉖**, a hulking, concrete monstrosity built in 1980 as a port and events centre. The structure is a fine example of Soviet design and excess. It's now undergoing a renovation and is expected to reopen in 2019.

KADRIORG

For Tallinn natives, the name 'Kadriorg' evokes images of nature, art and imperial Russian extravagance. This leafy neighbourhood of parks, ponds and villas just outside the city centre owes its existence to Tsar Peter the Great, who established a summer estate here in the early 18th century soon after conquering Estonia in the Great Northern War. He named the estate in honour of his wife, Catherine I, hence the name, which means 'Catherine's Valley' in Estonian.

In the 19th century, wealthy Tallinn residents began to build grand, wooden villas in the area, and in the 1920s and '30s, chic, functionalist houses started to appear. Through the years, the area kept its upper-class appeal, and it remains one of Tallinn's most prestigious neighbourhoods, as well as a favourite place to spend a relaxing afternoon, all the more so because it is now home to several of the nation's top art museums.

KADRIORG PALACE

The jewel in the Kadriorg's crown is the lavish, baroque **Kadriorg Palace** ㉗ (Kadrioru loss), built on the order of Peter the Great in 1718. Designed by Niccolo Michetti, an

Kadriorg Palace

Italian architect who also worked on the famous Peterhof near St Petersburg, the palace is laid out in Italian villa style – a main building flanked by two annexes. The tsar named it Ekaterinenthal, or Catherinenthal, in honour of his wife, and intended to use it as a summer residence, though in the end his family spent hardly any time here.

Its two-storey **main hall**, decorated with rich stuccowork and grandiose ceiling paintings, is considered one of the best examples of baroque design in Northern Europe. Behind the building, the carefully manicured, 18th-century-style **flower garden**, with its shooting fountains, is equally impressive.

As the building is itself a masterpiece, it is appropriate that it houses the **Kadriorg Art Museum** (https://kadriorumuuseum. ekm.ee; Wed 10am–8pm, May–Dec Wed 10am–8pm, Tue & Thu–Sun 10am–6pm, Jan–Apr Thu–Sun 10am–5pm), which exhibits

⊘ ROTERMANN QUARTER

By far the best place to see how Tallinn is putting a contemporary spin on its industrial heritage and breathing new life into once-rundown buildings is the Rotermann Quarter (Rotermanni Kvartal), located between Old Town and the Passenger Port. The former factory area has been thoroughly revamped into a shopping and culture zone complete with restaurants, galleries and a busy event area. The quarter's stylish, inventive architecture alone makes it worth a visit. While here, architecture buffs should also drop into the Rotermanni Salt Storage building at Ahtri 2. This distinctive example of a limestone building from 1908 houses the Museum of Estonian Architecture (www.arhitektuurimuuseum.ee; Wed–Fri 11am–6pm, Sat–Sun 10am–6pm), with rotating exhibitions.

the Estonian Art Museum's foreign art collection. Here precious paintings by Western European and Russian artists of the 16th–20th centuries are on display, as are prints, sculptures, superb works in metal and porcelain, and other creations.

While here, those interested in art should also visit the **Mikkel Museum** (https://mikkelimuuseum.ekm.ee; Wed 10am–8pm, May–Dec Tue, Thu–Sun 10am–6pm, Jan–Apr, Thu–Sun 10am–5pm), just across the street in what used to be the palace's kitchen building. Donated by a private collector, Johannes Mikkel, in 1994, the exquisite works include Flemish and Dutch paintings, Italian engravings and Chinese porcelain. The pride and joy of the collection is a set of four etchings by Rembrandt, one of which is a self-portrait.

Up the hill, just above the palace garden, is the Presidential Palace, the office and residence of Estonia's head of state. Built in 1938, this palace is relatively modest compared to its neighbour,

A ceiling fresco at Kadriorg Palace

the Kadriorg Palace, which had previously fulfilled this role. Though tourists aren't allowed inside, they may take photos of the exterior and of the honour guards standing at the front.

KUMU

At the top end of Weizenbergi stands the crème de la crème of all the city's art museums, the **Kumu** ㉘ (https://kumu.ekm. ee; Thu 10am–8pm, Tue–Wed and Fri–Sun 10am–6pm). Over a decade in the planning and building, this vast, high-tech art and culture centre opened in 2006 and serves as the main building of the Art Museum of Estonia. It focuses on Estonian art, displaying works by the nation's top creative talents through history.

The unique building itself makes a visit here worthwhile – designed by Finnish architect Pekka Vapaavuori and partially built into a limestone cliff, it looks like a work of science fiction brought to life, both inside and out.

KADRIORG PARK ATTRACTIONS

The sprawling **Kadriorg Park** ㉙ that surrounds Kadriorg Palace encompasses open spaces, wooded areas, statues, benches, paths and ponds.

By far the most dazzling of the park's sights is the large, rectangular **Swan Pond** adjacent to Weizenbergi Street, near the palace. The symmetrical pond with fountains and a beautiful, white gazebo at its centre could easily set the scene for a Tchaikovsky ballet. Here swans, ducks and pigeons all vie for the breadcrumbs that local children invariably throw, while their parents wander nearby, admiring the colourful flowerbeds that line the surrounding paths.

One of these paths leads southeast towards the Kumu, passing a children's play park before reaching a stairway and fountain area that is just as beautiful as the Swan Pond.

Over the street and running in front of the palace, a long, straight path leads towards the seashore, and to a magnificent statue of an angel, standing on a large stone pedestal, facing out to sea. This is the **Russalka** memorial, built to commemorate 177 men lost when the Russian warship *Russalka* sank en route from Tallinn to Helsinki in 1893. Russian-speaking couples traditionally lay flowers at the foot of this dramatic monument on their wedding day. From here, a 2km (3-mile) skate and bike path stretches along the rim of the bay, passing Maarjamäe and ending at Pirita Beach. Back over the wide road, slightly further down the coast, is the entrance to the **Song Festival Grounds** (Lauluväljak), home of Estonia's Song Festival, held every five years. It was here that the 'Singing Revolution' began (see page 23), when hundreds of thousands of Estonians gathered to sing traditional songs as a mass demonstration against Soviet dominance. The **Song Festival Arena**, with a distinctive, curving roof, was built in 1960 and is Tallinn's largest outdoor stage.

OUTLYING AREAS

MAARJAMÄE

This coastal hill just north of Kadriorg is a fascinating spot for visitors interested in World War II and Soviet history.

First and foremost, this is the site of the sprawling **Maarjamäe War Memorial** ③⓪, an impossibly ugly and over-bearing, cement-filled park that could only have been born of the Soviet 1960s and '70s. Its concrete avenues and abstract, iron sculptures were installed in 1975 to commemorate Soviet soldiers killed in Estonia during World War II. Many a semi-mandatory, enthusiastic Soviet rally was held at the now crumbling amphitheatre here. Ironically, the memorial is built on

A game of volleyball on Pirita Beach

what had earlier been a German cemetery, now marked by the solemn crosses visible behind the complex.

Nearby stands the **Maarjamäe Palace** (Maarjamäe loss), a grand, pseudo-Gothic manor built by Count Orlov-Davidov in 1874. Originally used as a summer home, the 'palace' changed hands several times through the years, serving as a Dutch consul's residence, a prestigious hotel, an aviation school and even a Soviet army barracks. The building now houses the branch of the **Estonian History Museum** (www.ajaloomuuseum.ee; Tue–Sun 10am–6pm) that focuses on the birth of the Estonian Republic, the occupation years and the second independence. It is also home to the **Estonian Film Museum**.

PIRITA

Pirita, a district 10 minutes' drive north of the centre, is Tallinn's favourite summer playground, mainly thanks to the immensely popular **Pirita Beach** ㉛, a vast stretch of sand invariably packed with tanning bodies and frolicking children on any warm day. The forested, mostly residential area also claims a number of other notable attractions, ranging from the captivatingly scenic to the grandly Soviet.

Squarely in the first category are the spectacular ruins of **St Bridget's Convent** ㉜ (Pirita klooster; www.piritaklooster. ee; daily Apr–Oct 10am–6pm, Jan–Dec noon–4pm). Founded by the Swedish Bridgettine Order in 1407, the convent operated here until Ivan the Terrible's forces destroyed it in 1577. What remains are the convent's towering, gabled facade, the walls of its main building, several foundations, cellars and a cemetery.

Beyond the ruins, the tranquil **Pirita River** slowly winds its way through the district before emptying out into Tallinn Bay. Pedal boats, rowing boats and canoes can be rented by the hour from **Pirita Boat Rental** (Paadilaenutus; http://bell

marine.ee; June–Aug daily 10am–10pm), operating from the built-up embankment, downhill from the convent. A leisurely row or pedalo ride is a perfect way to experience the lush, marshy beauty of the area.

In the Kloostrimetsa section of Pirita, about 3km (2 miles) from the beach, is a plant-lover's paradise, the **Tallinn Botanical Gardens** ③③ (Tallinna Botaanikaaed; www.botaani kaaed.ee; daily May–Sept 10am–8pm, greenhouses 11am–6pm, Oct–Apr 11am–5pm, greenhouses 11am–4pm). More than 8,000 plant species can be found on its 123 hectares (300 acres) of landscaped grounds and its greenhouses display everything from rare varieties to houseplants.

Joint tickets are available for the Botanical Gardens and this area's other main attraction, the space-age-looking **Tallinn TV Tower** ③④ (Teletorn; www.teletorn.ee; daily 10am–6pm). The gargantuan structure dates to the Soviet 1980s but was given a thorough update for its 2012 reopening. At 314m (1,030ft), it is by far the tallest structure in town. You may have to queue at peak times before boarding the super-fast lift to the observation deck at the 175m (575ft) level, but it is worth the wait. Unforgettable, 360-degree views of the city and surrounding ports unfold from here, and those who don't suffer from vertigo are even encouraged to stand on patches of glass flooring. The tower also features a brasserie-style café-restaurant, a 3D film, an exhibition about the tower's history and another about world-famous Estonians.

OPEN AIR MUSEUM

Rocca al Mare, once a private, seaside estate on the western edge of Kopli Bay, is now home to one of Tallinn's most unique tourist attractions, the **Estonian Open Air Museum** ③⑤ (Eesti Vabaõhumuuseum; www.evm.ee; daily 23 Apr–Sept

10am–8pm, houses and tavern until 6pm, Oct–22 Apr 10am–5pm]. Dozens of thatch-roofed 18th–20th century farmhouses, barns, windmills and watermills combine to give a vivid impression of what Estonian village life must have been like in times past. Characters dressed in period costume drive horse carts through the park, others perform chores in the various buildings while visitors

Reconstruction of traditional windmills at the Estonian Open Air Museum

look on. One of the mandatory stops here is the Kolu Tavern, famous for its traditional Estonian pea soup.

Visitors should set aside at least half a day to tour the park properly. Those with children in tow should also note that the **Tallinn Zoo** (see page 94) is in the same part of town.

EXCURSIONS

A day trip from Tallinn will allow you to experience the rugged splendour of Estonia's countryside or explore one of the nation's other notable cities, each of which has a history and spirit quite different from those of the capital. For visitors with more time on their hands, hiring a car is a good way to see the country. That said, it is not essential; convenient buses connect Tallinn to the cities mentioned here, and for the more out-of-the-way locations organised tours are available.

A pretty forest near Käsmu

LAHEMAA NATIONAL PARK

Along the northern coast about an hour's drive east of Tallinn
lies Estonia's largest nature reserve, **Lahemaa National Park**
(Lahemaa rahruspark), a perfect antidote to urban tourism. The
725 sq km (280 sq mile) park encompasses vast areas of forest, jagged seashores, wetlands and several historic villages,
as well as some stunning 17th–18th-century manor houses.

Your first stop should be **Palmse Manor** (Palmse Mõis), the
most striking manor house in the country. Completed in 1740, it
was home to the von der Pahlen family until 1919, when a land
reform law nationalised the manorial holdings and divided them
among local farmers. The house then served as a convalescent
home and later a Soviet pioneer camp, but it has since been renovated and now operates as a museum (www.palmse.ee; daily
10am–6pm). Visitors are welcome to stroll the manor grounds,
where they'll find a peaceful swan pond and landscaped gardens.

The manor also serves as Lahemaa's **Visitor Centre** (http://loodusegakoos.ee; mid May–mid Sept daily 9am–5pm, mid Sep–mid May Mon–Fri 9am–5pm). In the stable-carriage house you'll find maps and information on the park's sights and nature walks.

Not far away is another impressive manor house, **Sagadi Manor**, now a hotel. It was built in 1749, but renovated at the end of that century in a neoclassical style. As with Palmse, the complex is open to visitors and its interior contains a museum. One of its outbuildings also houses a forestry museum (http://sagadi.ee/museum).

Lahemaa's other attractions include several hamlets, such as **Altja**, a lovely Estonian fishing village. The old wooden buildings here were restored in the 1970s, and the village has since become a popular local tourist spot. Here you'll find a 19th-century inn, a traditional village swing and several paths along the coast.

Another coastal village, **Käsmu**, is less typical. This one has a decidedly affluent look as a result of its residents' salt-smuggling activities in the 19th century. In the 1920s, when Finland imposed prohibition, the economic focus here naturally shifted to alcohol. Apart from the houses of wealthy sea

The swan pond at Palmse Manor

captains, Käsmu is known for its **Maritime Museum** (free), housed in what was once a school of navigation.

Like Käsmu, the village of **Viinistu** also profited from alcohol smuggling, but what puts it on the map nowadays is something else entirely. This village of just 150 people is home to the **Viinistu Art Museum** (http://www.viinistu.ee/site; daily 11am– 6pm, mid Sep –May closed Mon–Tue), which has the largest private art collection in Estonia. The 19th- and 20th-century Estonian paintings on display easily rival those of the state-owned museums in Tallinn. This anomaly is thanks to one former resident who, as a child, fled with his family to Sweden during World War II. After making his fortune as manager of the pop group ABBA, he returned to Viinistu, eventually converting a Soviet-era fish collective into this art centre. Apart from the museum, the village has a respectable tavern and a small trail that follows the coastline.

JÄGALA WATERFALL

On the way to Lahemaa, visitors can take a small detour north from the Narva Highway to the village of Jägala-Joa, home to one of Estonia's best-known beauty spots, the **Jägala Waterfall ㊱**. About 8m (26ft) high and at times as much as 70m (230ft) wide, the waterfall is given its uniquely spectacular look by the way the river pours over the edge of a perfectly flat limestone shelf. The exposed cliff face reveals more layers of limestone, a geological feature for which northern Estonia is famous. Through the centuries, the waterfall has cut a gorge that is 300m (980ft) long and 12–14m (39–46ft) deep.

NAISSAAR, AEGNA AND PRANGLI

Strictly summer destinations, these three forested islands off the Tallinn coast offer opportunities to experience the serenity of

The spectacular Jagala Waterfall

Estonian nature as well as glimpse some truly curious aspects of the nation's past. Visiting each requires planning and is best done with the help of a tour operator. The most easily accessible is **Naissaar**, or 'Women's Island', about 10km (6 miles) from the mainland. Tallinn-Cruises.com (tel: 514 5118) operates the twice-daily ferry and offers tours (summer only).

Since the late 1990s most of the island has been a nature reserve, but for nearly 50 years it was a closed Soviet naval base whose main function was the manufacture of sea mines.

Military sites around the island include the abandoned mine factory, a ghost town that once housed Soviet military personnel, and the remains of concrete bunkers. Trails also take visitors to the island's two **lighthouses**, and past **cemeteries** where English and French soldiers from the Crimean War are buried.

The island is 11km (7 miles) long and 4km (2.5 miles) wide and can be explored on foot or by bicycle (rental at the dock).

The **Nature Park Centre**, uphill from the dock, provides maps to the two main **trails**.

The island's only village, **Männiku**, is about 20 minutes' walk from the port and has a restaurant and guesthouse. From here, a narrow-gauge railway operates for tourists.

Aegna, Tallinn's 'picnic island', is a quarter of the size of Naissaar and was also militarised during the Soviet period. Its main attraction is now its tranquillity, with hiking trails, beaches, an old cemetery and a 'magical stone maze' among its prominent features. Operated by Kihnu Veeteed (www.veeteed.com; tel: 443 1069), the ferry Juku makes the one-hour crossing from Tallinn's Kalasadam (summer only).

Unlike the other two islands, **Prangli** was spared from wartime depopulation. Thanks to this, it has been able to preserve a traditional fishing culture with roots going back six centuries. In addition to seeing what village life is like for the island's 150 residents, visitors are treated to pristine beaches, pine forests and a museum. Prangli Tours (www.tallinndaytrip.com; tel: 555 37 819) runs full-service excursions (summer only).

Fragile waters

Because the Baltic Sea is virtually enclosed by land it is environmentally extremely sensitive. It takes around 35 years for all of the water in the sea to be replaced by water from the ocean beyond. If any pollutants enter the water, they will stay there for two or three decades, by which time they may have severely damaged the area's ecosystems.

PÄRNU

Each year, when the seasons change and the weather finally starts to turn warm, Estonians like to abandon their dreary offices and schoolrooms and head off to **Pärnu** ③⑦, their 'summer capital', on a coastal inlet 129km (80 miles) south of

Tallinn. This quiet resort town of more than 51,000 inhabitants is known for its leafy parks, health spas, quaint town centre and, most of all, its long stretch of white sandy beach.

Though Pärnu is more than 750 years old and has seen numerous changes of empire, its most relevant history starts in 1838, when the town's first health spa was established. Thanks to the curative properties of the

Pärnu, Tallinn's summer capital

town's mud treatments, relatively warm weather and sea air, Pärnu quickly grew into a popular spa destination – a tradition that continues today. Now it can claim six spa hotels offering everything from plastic surgery to water slides.

When most travellers first arrive in Pärnu, they find themselves in the historic downtown area, the centrepiece of which is **Rüütli Street**. This long, pedestrian walkway and the few streets that surround it are home to numerous cafés, boutiques and a hotchpotch of intriguing buildings dating from the 17th to 20th centuries. The most impressive of these landmarks are the imposing **Eliisabeti Church** from 1747, the dazzling Orthodox **Ekateriina Church** from 1768, and the mid-17th-century **Almshouse** (Seegi maja), which now operates as a hotel and restaurant. Another notable 17th-century structure, the **Tallinn Gate** (Tallinna väravad), marks what used to be the road to Tallinn before the Pärnu River was finally spanned in 1938.

The pink Town Hall in Tartu

Pärnu's oldest building is the **Red Tower** (Punane torn), a squat, 15th-century tower that once guarded the edge of town. Now painted white, it is hidden in an alley adjacent to Hommiku Street.

A couple of blocks north of the historic area, at Aida 3, stands the **Pärnu Museum** (www.parnu muuseum.ee; Tue–Sun 10am–6pm). With its modern exhibits, it offers a good introduction to the history of the town's development. Ringing downtown on the south and east is a well-developed park and marina area. Its flowerbeds, fountains and numerous paths make it an excellent place to relax or stroll. On the streets nearby you can find several examples of old, wooden villas and functionalist houses from the prewar period.

A few minutes' walk south brings you to Pärnu's true centre of gravity – the **beach**. Cafés, volleyball nets, ice-cream vendors, lifeguards and all the other trappings of a typical, world-class beach can be found here. The only things lacking are crashing waves and sharks. When you tire of bronzing yourself on the sand, you can take time to see the area's treasures. The **Beach House** (Rannahoone), with a distinctive, mushroom-shaped balcony, dates from 1939 and is a wonderful example of functionalism. The same can be said of the striking **Beach Hotel** (Rannahotell; www.rannahotell.ee) nearby, completed in 1937.

Though now empty, the neoclassical **Pärnu Mud Bath** building (Pärnu Mudaravila), with a dome-shaped roof and circular garden, remains a symbol of the town, as does the luxury hotel and restaurant **Ammende Villa**, (http://ammende.ee) housed in an art nouveau mansion slightly further away down Mere Puiestee.

Also adjacent to the beach is the **Beach Park** (Rannapark), established in 1882. You can slowly meander through the park and contemplate the scenery, or hire a pair of roller skates at the beach and rocket along its many paved paths.

TARTU

Its nickname is 'the city of good thoughts', but a better name for **Tartu** ③⑧, a minor metropolis 189km (118 miles) southeast of Tallinn, might be 'the city of good ideas'. Tartu is Estonia's intellectual capital, home not only to the nation's largest and most prestigious educational institution, Tartu University, but also to several colleges, research centres and the nation's supreme court.

The atmosphere here is decidedly different from that in Tallinn – less rushed, more contemplative and, thanks to its student population, visibly younger. With 99,000 inhabitants, this is Estonia's second-largest city, but Tartu is still small enough to lack the annoyances found in many urban areas. At the same time it has a number of cafés, parks, museums and historic sites that are just as interesting as any you could find in the capital.

As in Tallinn, the heart of Tartu is its **Old Town**, where the city's most striking architecture is concentrated. Unlike Tallinn, though, Tartu's Old Town no longer has a medieval look – constant wars during the 17th century and the Great Fire of 1775 mean that most of what you see here was built in the late 18th and 19th centuries. Your first Old Town destination should be **Town Hall Square** (Raekoja plats), the centre of Tartu from time immemorial. The **Town Hall** (Raekoda) presiding over the top of the square was opened in 1786 and its design reflects a mixture of early classicism, baroque and rococo. The building is home to the **Tourist Information** office. The mischievous fountain directly in front of the Town Hall, ***Kissing Students***, is a relatively recent installation, but has already become a favourite symbol of the town.

Further down the square is Tartu's Leaning Tower of Pisa, the **Tartu Art Museum** (www.tartmus.ee; Wed and Fri–Sun 11am–6pm, Thu 11am–9pm), which tilts bizarrely to the left due to the soft riverbank mud on which it stands. The nearby **arched bridge** over the Emajõgi River replaced the 18th-century stone bridge that was destroyed in 1944. Taking a daring walk over the arched bridge's top rail has become a student tradition.

Just off the square from the Town Hall you'll find one of the most outstanding examples of neoclassical architecture in Estonia, the **Tartu University Main Building**. The Swedish King Gustav Adolph established Tartu University in 1632, and this structure was completed in 1809. The building houses an impressive concert hall, an art museum (Mon–Fri 11am–6pm; charge) whose collection of antiquities includes a 4,000-year-old Egyptian mummy, and a Student Lock-up, where students were incarcerated for bad conduct. Not far away is Old Town's principal church, **St John's Church** (Jaani Kirik), which dates back to the late 12th century and is renowned for its more than 1,000 terracotta figures.

A short climb up **Toome Hill** (Toomemägi) brings you to the towering brick ruins of **Dome Cathedral**. Built in the 13th century, the cathedral served as the centre of a regional bishopric prior to the Reformation. Fire destroyed it in 1624. A restored section now houses the extensive **Museum of Tartu University History** (www.ajaloomuuseum.ut.ee; Wed–Sun 11am–5pm), which displays old lab equipment, photos and the like. Some of the cathedral towers are also open for exploration April to November. On another crest of the hill stands Tartu's **Old Observatory**

(May–Sep Tue–Sun 10am–6pm, Oct–Apr Wed–Sun 11am–5pm), which began operation in 1810 and housed the most advanced telescope of its time. It now operates as a museum, displaying antique star-gazing devices and an old-fashioned planetarium show. Visitors can turn the rotating dome roof and climb outside for city views. Afterwards, they can stop for a pint at the nearby **Vilde Lokaal** (Vallikraavi 4),

Kissing Students fountain in Town Hall Square

a richly decorated haunt in a historic printing house. A statue in front of the pub depicts a fictional chance meeting of Oscar Wilde (1854–1900) and the Estonian writer Eduard Wilde (1865–1933) on a park bench. An identical monument, a gift from Estonia in 2004, can be found in central Galway.

For travellers with children, no visit to Tartu would be complete without a trip to the high-tech **AHHAA Science Centre** (www.ahhaa.ee; Sun–Thu 10am–7pm, Fri–Sat 10am–8pm), a vast complex filled with clever, hands-on experiments and activities.

HAAPSALU

Haapsalu ⑨, a seaside town 101km (63 miles) southwest of Tallinn, gives an insight into small-town life in Estonia. Early 20th-century wooden houses dominate Haapsalu's central neighbourhoods, many of its narrow streets have never been paved, and its residents seem to amble about in a particularly unhurried manner. At the same time, this resort town, which competes with Pärnu for the title of having the nation's most therapeutic mud, is home to enough historic curiosities to make a trip here worthwhile for anyone with a day to spare.

Haapsalu's best-known attraction is the late 13th-century **Episcopal Castle** that dominates the town centre. The castle served as both religious outpost and military fortress until Peter the Great conquered it at the beginning of the 18th century. Though it mostly lies in ruins, much of the structure is still intact and visitors are free to stroll through its grassy courtyard and examine its remaining walls and old cannons. In summer one section operates as a **museum** (www.salm.ee; museum closed for renovation at the time of writing, grounds open daily 7am–midnight) chronicling the town's history. When the museum is

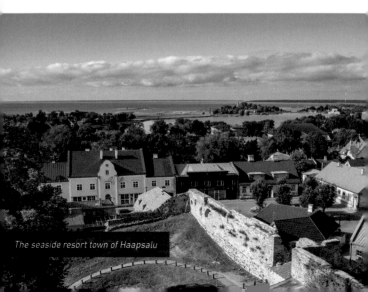

The seaside resort town of Haapsalu

open, visitors can also pay to climb the castle's **watchtower**, from where there's a magnificent view.

One part of the castle that's not in ruins is the **Haapsalu Dome Church**, whose beautiful interior you can see if you tour the castle's museum. One of the church's windows is central to the town's favourite legend, 'The White Lady of Haapsalu'. The ghostly figure of a woman, who was supposedly immured in the castle walls, is said to appear on the window on moonlit nights in August. An annual White Lady Days music festival is named after the legend.

Mud matters

People from all over the world come looking for cures from Haapsalu's sea mud. News of its efficacy was spread by Carl Abraham Hunnius, a military doctor who founded the first mud treatment centre here in 1825. It wasn't long before the fashionable folk of St Petersburg were making their way to Haapsalu.

Not far from here is the town's seaside **promenade**, a good place for a stroll. Here you'll see a grand-looking, wooden **Resort Hall** (Kuursaal), which operates as a restaurant in summer. Next to it is a **stone bench** that, with the help of modern technology, talks and plays classical music. This is a monument to the composer Pyotr Tchaikovsky, who supposedly got the inspiration for Swan Lake while resting in Haapsalu.

Rail enthusiasts should head to the **Estonian Railway Museum** (www.salm.ee; Sep–Apr Fri–Sun 11am–4pm, May–Aug daily 10am–6pm). Built into Haapsalu's romantic, early 20th-century railway station, the small museum displays a replica stationmaster's room, passenger's waiting room and a number of tools and uniforms. Outside on the tracks is a collection of locomotives and engines from the 1940s and '50s.

Shopping at a flea market

WHAT TO DO

ENTERTAINMENT

During the height of the tourist season, live, outdoor entertainment is not just easy to find in Tallinn, it is nearly impossible to escape. Every kind of music, from traditional Estonian folk to Scottish bagpipes, echoes through the air as small, seemingly impromptu concerts erupt on squares and street corners in the Old Town.

The most uniquely Estonian events are those involving national song and dance. Generally these folk performances are held only when specific festivals are scheduled, but if you happen to see groups of women wearing brightly striped village skirts, follow them to their concert and you will be rewarded with beautiful, rural music traditions that go back hundreds of years.

CLASSICAL MUSIC, OPERA AND BALLET

Estonia's national concert organiser, Eesti Kontsert (https://concert.ee), acts as a kind of one-stop-shop for Tallinn's classical performances. The company sells tickets for a whole spectrum of classical entertainment from its box office in the **Estonia Concert Hall** (Estonia pst. 4; tel: 6147 705; Mon–Fri noon–9pm). Opera (www.opera.ee/en) and ballet tickets are sold in another part of the same building. Larger classical events take place in the theatre itself or in the nearby **Nordea Concert Hall** (www.tallinnconcerthall.com), while medieval churches, guildhalls and towers provide interesting venues for the smaller performances. **Modern dance performances** take place in the Kanuti Guildhall (Pikk 20; www.saal.ee).

For a change from the usual *Swan Lake* and *La Traviata*, buy tickets to any show given by Tallinn's early music ensemble, **Hortus Musicus**, whose repertoire of baroque and Renaissance music fits in well with the city's historic ambience. **Organ Concerts**, held every Saturday and Sunday afternoon in St Nicholas's Church (Niguliste 3; admission with the museum ticket), offer a more casual, classical performance option. Concert times are posted outside the church.

POP AND ROCK MUSIC

The city's small but lively band scene mainly revolves around its bars and clubs (see below), but every so often stand-alone concerts take place, usually in connection with some kind of music festival. Also, major international stars visit Tallinn when their current tour brings them to this part of Europe. In both cases, advertisements all around the city will make sure you know what is going on.

To see what the events are before you make your trip, check the Piletilevi ticket agency's website (www.piletilevi.ee), which also gives you information about tickets and lets you book them online.

Concerts galore

In summer you will find a classical concert or dance performance in Tallinn just about every night of the week. For an up-to-date list of what is happening on the cultural front, check the city tourist office's homepage (www.visittallinn.ee).

CINEMA

Cinema is an easy entertainment option in Tallinn as films are nearly always shown in their original language, with Estonian subtitles. The 11-screen Coca-Cola Plaza (Hobujaama 5; www.forumcinemas.ee) screens mainly Hollywood fare, as does the Solaris Kino

(Estonia pst. 9; www.sola-ris.ee). The Sõprus (Vana-Posti 8; www.kinosoprus.ee) and Artis (Estonia pst. 9; www.kino.ee) concentrate on art-house films. Phone 1182 or check www.1182.ee for all show times and information in English.

NIGHTLIFE

There is absolutely no bet-ter way to relax in Tallinn than to sit in an outdoor café, beer in hand, watch-

Women in traditional Estonian folk outfits

ing the world slowly meander past. Fortunately, the city also has a wide spectrum of nightlife to explore – everything from quiet, sophisticated lounges to pulsing dance clubs.

Like everything else in Tallinn, most of the nightlife is squeezed into the Old Town streets, giving rise to the custom of frequent bar-hopping. Since the bars are literally only a few paces apart, locals (and savvy visitors) will often change loca-tions after every single drink, exploring all the options until they finally choose a place to settle in.

The bar-packed area around Suur-Karja and Väike-Karja becomes party central at weekends, with crowds, noise and drinks spilling out onto the streets. **Nimeta Baar** (Suur-Karja 4; https://nimetabaar.ee) is at the centre of the action and is popular among the young, tourist set. Beer aficionados should head to the **Drink Baar & Grill** (Väike-Karja 8), where over 80 carefully selected brews are available. More local flavour can

Spoilt for choice at the knitwear market

be found at the ever-popular **Hell Hunt** (Pikk 39), which has a good atmosphere and its own brand of beer.

For trendy, lounge-type surroundings, the **Deja Vu** (Vana-Viru 8; www.dejavu.ee) and **Butterfly Lounge** (Vana-Viru 13; http://kokteilibaar.ee) are both good choices. Cosy wine bars have also become fashionable. Two highly recommended wine bars are **Il Gallo Nero** (Rataskaevu 4) and the old-fashioned, chic **Gloria Veinikelder** (Müürivahe 2; https://gloriaveinikelder.ee).

Many of the larger bars and pubs offer live music at weekends, but some venues are particularly sought out for their entertainment offerings. **Clayhills Gastropub** (Pikk 13) serves up jazz and other types of music most nights, while **Von Krahli Baar** (Rataskaevu 10; www.vonkrahl.ee) is the place to go for alternative parties.

Nightclubs are also easy to find, but hard to recommend. Crowds are fickle, so what could be full of life on one night could be desolate the next. One that is always popular, however, is the huge, central **Club Hollywood** (Vana-Posti 8; http://clubhollywood. ee), which draws a young crowd. The scene at nearby **Vabank** (Harju 13; http://vabank.ee/en/) is more exclusive and mature.

SHOPPING

The explosive growth in Tallinn's retail sector over the past decade means you will have absolutely no trouble stuffing your suitcase with gifts, souvenirs and other goodies. More shops and boutiques blossom with each new tourist season, and several shopping malls crowd the downtown area. What's more, all but the smallest locations will happily accept your plastic.

Despite these huge improvements in the shopping culture, however, Estonia is still a fairly secluded market, which means that not everything here is a bargain. Clothes, for example, can actually cost more in Tallinn than in relatively rich Scandinavia. Likewise, electronics are rarely a good deal. The upshot is that you cannot assume that things are cheaper here, and comparing prices to what you would pay at home is crucial if you want to avoid spending blunders.

Nevertheless, with some types of products, you can almost always find good value. Anything made locally, particularly handicrafts, art and Estonian-produced fashion, is a safe bet. Additionally, alcohol and cigarettes are typically a steal here because Estonia does not tax these items nearly as much as

Laughs for sale

Expat-run Comedy Estonia organises frequent, English-speaking stand-up events in pubs and clubs where aspiring locals, as well as foreign guest acts, work the crowds. See www.comedyestonia. com for the schedule.

neighbouring countries do. This explains why Finnish beer is so much cheaper in Estonia than in Finland, and why the ferry back to Helsinki is always crowded with bleary-eyed karaoke stars.

WHERE TO SHOP

Without doubt, the Old Town holds the most promise for the intrepid souvenir hunter. This area has by far the highest concentration of shops specialising in linen, glass, ceramics, knitwear and other authentic, locally made wares. Similarly, establishments offering antiques, art and traditional handicrafts line just about every street, especially those nearest Town Hall Square. General *suveniir* stores will sell the classic T-shirts and postcards, and are often crammed with mass-produced Russian dolls and the like. In short, almost anywhere you are in the Old Town, you will be able to find shopping within a few metres.

Outdoor markets, while not actually common in Tallinn, present the most interesting shopping experience. First and foremost is the much-loved **knitwear market** along the old city wall on Müürivahe Street, near the Viru Gates. Since it does not have an official name, most foreigners simply refer to it as the **Sweater Wall**. Here, local women sell just about every kind of knitted item you can imagine, with a better variation in styles than in most shops. A similar, but less spectac-ular craft market operates nearby on Mere Puiestee, just north of Vana-Viru Street. In summer, tempo-rary markets also appear from week to week on or near Town Hall Square, where there is an enchant-ing **Christmas Market**.

Bartering

Market vendors may give you a small discount for buying in volume, but gen-erally they do not barter. The price they quote is what they expect to get.

An equally fascinating place to pick up a gift or two is the **Katariina Guild**, in St Catherine's Passage (Katariina käik), which runs from the Sweater Wall to Vene Street. In this string of small workshops, visitors can watch craftswomen at work creating quilts, ceramics, glass items, jewellery, hats and hand-painted silk. While the artists use time-honoured methods, their products are usually modern, even avant-garde.

The more traditional Estonian handicraft items are available in any souvenir shop, but the most authentic and interesting are sold by **Eesti Käsitöö** (Estonian Handicraft; http://folkart. ee/en), which operates shops on Pikk 22, Vene 12, Lühike Jälg 6a and in the Viru Centre. Here you can find everything from dolls and wooden toys to entire Estonian folk costumes.

Shoppers looking for everyday fashions and other non-souvenir items will find the best selection in large department stores and malls outside the Old Town. The most notable of these are the **Viru Centre** (http://virukeskus. com/en) and the attached **Kaubamaja** department store, both in central Tallinn next to Viru Square. Tallinn's branch of **Stockmann** (www.stockmann.ee), the esteemed Finnish department store, is a short walk from there at Liivalaia 53. Other good shopping centres, such as the **Kristiine Centre** (www.kristiinekeskus.ee) and the **Ülemiste Centre** (www.ulemiste.ee), can be reached by taxi.

WHAT TO BUY

Handicrafts, in all shapes and forms, are still the undisputed rulers of the city's souvenir world, thanks to modern Estonia's strong connection to its rural past. **Knitted items**, such as woollen jumpers, mittens, gloves, socks and hats, top the list in popularity. Most of the knitwear is created in typical Estonian or Nordic patterns. A particularly fun variation sold here is a ridiculously long woollen cap, the drooping end of which is supposed to be tied around the neck like a scarf. Almost as common as knitwear is **linen**, which has been produced here since medieval times. A huge variety of linen articles is available, ranging from tablecloths to dresses.

Anything made of **carved wood**, particularly the fragrant juniper, is also a popular Estonian souvenir. Toys, dolls, beer mugs, butter knives and countless other wooden handicrafts sold in the shops make excellent and inexpensive gifts.

Though it actually comes from Lithuania and Poland, **amber** has become a pan-Baltic souvenir, and many visitors feel obliged to pick up at least one piece of amber jewellery when visiting Tallinn. Apart from its well-known light-caramel colour, it can also be found in white, green and a deep brown.

Antiques of all sorts are widely sold throughout the Old Town. Antique furniture, gramophones, Russian icons and the like are available, though buyers should be aware of the restrictions on exporting items made before 1945 (see page 133). Even for non-collectors, browsing one of the low-end antique shops can be an adventure as they are typically packed with unique **Soviet-era trinkets**.

Estonia has also become known for its **cutting-edge fashion** and **home-decor** scene, with designers selling their offbeat creations from speciality boutiques around town. These items often have an artsy, Nordic look.

One souvenir that says 'Tallinn' like no other is **Vana Tallinn liqueur**, available in any alcohol shop for a modest price. The sweet, dark liquid can be sipped as-is from a shot glass or, better still, added to coffee or ice cream. Bottles of Vana Tallinn are often sold in linen satchels, making them very presentable as

Beaded jewellery made of amber

gifts. Finally, just as sweet as the liqueur but far less hazardous are **chocolates**, either those made by Tallinn's famous Kalev confectionery company, available in nicely decorated boxes, or the exquisite hand-made chocolates sold in speciality cafés in the Old Town.

SPORTS

As in most European countries, football is king among spectator sports. Both the national team and Tallinn's *Meistriliiga* (top-league) club FC Flora play their home games in the A. Le Coq Arena (Asula 4c; tel: 6279 940).

Basketball enjoys nearly equal popularity, with Tallinn's Kalev/Cramo the most recognised of the handful of teams based around the country. Both the Kalev/Cramo and the national team play their games in the Saku Suurhall (Paldiski

Skiing

In Estonia, skiing is second nature. Every February thousands set out on the gruelling 63km (39-mile) Tartu Marathon. The cross-country race is part of the international Worldloppet series, and attracts competitors from around the world.

mnt. 104B; tel: 6600 200; www.sakusuurhall.ee).

Fans who want to watch their home team's rugby or football match on satellite TV should head to Old Town pubs such as **Nimeta** (Suur-Karja 4) or **Clayhills** (Pikk 13; www.clayhills.ee), both of which have large screens and plenty of beer and snacks.

Swimming is possible year-round thanks to several indoor pools around the city. Among the most easily accessible is the pool at the Kalev Spa Hotel & Water Park (Aia 18; tel: 6493 370; www.kalevspa.ee). In summer, however, **Pirita Beach** provides a decent, if crowded, place to get wet. The more adventurous can even try their hand at Estonia's favourite water sport – **windsurfing**. The Battery Pirita Surfclub (tel: 569 88 093; www.surf.ee) offers four-hour lessons for beginners, with equipment and wetsuits provided.

Tallinn's nearest **golf** centre is the Estonian Golf & Country Club (tel: 6025 290; www.egcc.ee), about 25 minutes' drive from town, which features an 18-hole course by the sea. **Squash** players can head to Metro Squash (Tondi 17; tel: 6556 392), which also rents equipment. **Tennis** clubs in Tallinn are also visitor-friendly. Good choices are the Rocca al Mare Tennis Centre (Haabersti 5; tel: 6600 540; http://tenniseklubi.ee) and the Kalevi Tenniseklubi (Herne 28; tel: 6459 229; www.kalevitenniseklubi.ee).

In winter, **ice-skating** is a great choice for outdoor fun. At the Harju Ice Rink (tel: 5624 6739; www.uisuplats.ee), in the park along Harju Street, you can glide around to music while taking in the Old Town surroundings.

CHILDREN

Tallinn does not offer too many obvious activities for children, but with a little strategic planning, you should have no trouble keeping the smile on any young face.

The most fun way to tour the Old Town in summer is hitching a ride on **Toomas the Train**. The red-and-black electric, track-less train departs from Kullassepa (near the Town Hall) and makes a 20-minute circuit through the cobblestone streets. The **bicycle taxis** operating in the centre also provide an amusing option for getting around.

Among the main child-oriented attractions in Old Town is the **NUKU Museum of Puppet Arts** (Lai 1; www.nuku.ee; Tue–Sun 10am–6pm), an extensive and high-tech display of the

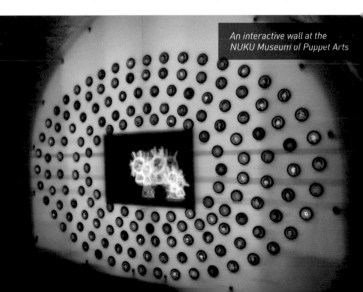

An interactive wall at the NUKU Museum of Puppet Arts

creatures created by the well-loved **Estonian Puppet Theatre**. Not far away, the 15th-century **Epping Tower** (Laboratooriumi 31; www.epping.ee; May–15 Sept Thur–Tue 10am–6pm, 16 Sept–April Sat–Sun 11am–4pm) introduces the medieval era with several floors of hands-on exhibits. Here young visitors are even invited to try on chain mail and armour.

For those with a sweet tooth, there's the **Kalev Chocolate Shop and Sweets Mastery** (Roseni 7; www.kalev.eu; Mon–Sat 10am–8pm, Sun 11am–6pm), which displays over 200 marzipan creations and offers workshops on how to make marzipan and figurines.

After strolling through the Kadriorg district and feeding the ducks at the Swan Pond, visit the **Miia-Milla-Manda Museum** (Koidula 21C; www.linnamuuseum.ee; Tue–Sun noon–6pm). Aimed at children aged from 3 to 11, it offers plenty of imaginative activities, as well as an outdoor play park.

Farther out, the **Tallinn Zoo** (Paldiski mnt. 145; www.tallinnzoo.ee; daily May–Aug 10am–7pm, Mar–Apr and Sept–Oct 10am–6pm, Nov–Feb 10am–4pm) never fails to enthral young visitors. More than 350 species of animals, including wolves, tigers, bears, elephants and lynx, make their home here. Older children will want to head out to the **FK Centre** (Paldiski mnt. 229a; www.fkkeskus.ee; Apr–Oct Mon–Fri 2pm–8pm, Sat–Sun noon–9pm), where they can engage in a laser shoot-out or live out their Formula-1 fantasies on the high-speed, motorised go-cart track.

Pirita Beach is a popular destination for family fun in the warm season, but no matter what time of year, kids can make a splash at the centrally located, indoor **Kalev Spa Water Park** (Aia 18; www.kalevspa.ee; closed for renovation at the time of writing), which has water slides as well as bubble baths and kiddie pools.

CALENDAR OF EVENTS

Tallinn hosts a number of festivals throughout the year, most of them centred on music and dance performances or designed to showcase the city's medieval past. In this extreme climate, events are carefully scheduled to take account of the season, though jazz festivals, dance festivals and classical concert cycles might happen at any time of year. Visitors may also be interested in major festivals going on in nearby towns. Big draws are the Watergate World Music festival in Pärnu in July and the popular Viljandi Folk Festival, hosted in late July in the historic, southern town of Viljandi.

1 January New Year's fireworks on Freedom Square.

March Tallinn Music Week (https://tmw.ee): the nation's top musical acts showcase their talent (late March).

April Jazzkaar (www.jazzkaar.ee/en): international jazz festival, featuring world-class performers from Estonia and abroad (late April).

June Old Town Days Festival (http://vanalinnapaevad.ee): entertaining mix of medieval tournaments, markets and concerts all over the Old Town (first week of June).

July Beer Summer: the season's largest outdoor party. Four days of beer tasting and concerts by Estonia's top bands (early July). Tallinn Maritime Days: a weekend of boat-themed, family entertainment at the harbours.

July–August International Organ Festival (late July or early August; www.festivals.ee).

August Birgitta Festival (www.filharmoonia.ee/en/birgitta): a week-long, modern musical theatre festival against the backdrop of the Pirita Convent ruins (mid-August). August Dance: modern dance performances by cutting-edge groups from Estonia and abroad.

November–December Black Nights Film Festival (https://blacknights filmfestival.com): international feature films, with sub-festivals for student films, children's films and animation (two weeks, beginning late November or early December).

December Christmas Market in Town Hall Square (throughout the month). Advent concerts in churches throughout town.

EATING OUT

With such a variety of dining options available in Tallinn – from romantic cellar cafés to exotic ethnic restaurants – eating out can be every bit as exciting as exploring the medieval capital itself. The Old Town in particular is so full of competing establishments that many have taken to having staff, sometimes in medieval or theme costumes, patrolling the streets to lure in would-be customers with leaflets and coupons.

Eating out is a relative bargain. Full meals in restaurants can easily be found for as little as €10–12 per person. Even the most exclusive establishments will charge only around €25 for a main course. Beware, however, of the outdoor cafés along Viru Street and on Town Hall Square, many of which fall under the 'tourist trap' classification, with their high prices, slow service and mediocre food.

MEAL TIMES

Breakfast is typically served between 7 and 10am on weekdays, and as late as noon at weekends. Restaurants are open for lunch at 11am or noon for the odd early customer, though lunch breaks peak between 1 and 2pm. Dinner crowds fill restaurants between 6.30 and 8pm on weekdays, shifting to about an hour later on Friday and Saturday evenings. Late diners should note that restaurants stop serving food around 10 or 11pm, but some pubs in the Old Town will keep their kitchens open until midnight or later.

BREAKFAST

Nearly all hotels include breakfast in the price of the room. Depending on the establishment, this could be anything from a bread roll with cheese and a cup of coffee to

Eating out in the Old Town

an extensive breakfast buffet with five types of juice. The Estonian breakfast differs little from its typical continental European counterpart; eggs, sausage, muesli, cornflakes and yoghurt are the mainstays.

Local additions include the ever-popular porridge, as well as dark bread and slices of tomato, cucumber and cheese for making sandwiches. Chunks of herring are often available in many breakfast buffets.

Outside the hotels, a full breakfast is hard to find as few restaurants open before 11am. A number of pubs indeed offer a 'full English breakfast served all day' for the weekend party crowds, but don't expect them to open their doors any earlier.

An excellent alternative for anyone who wants to get an early bite is to visit one of the many bakeries in the city centre and Old Town. These usually open at 7 or 8am, and serve a huge variety of fresh pastries, croissants and cakes, along with coffee and tea. Most have a few small tables available for customers who want to enjoy their pastries on the spot. In the Old Town, these bakeries can be recognised by the traditional, pretzel-shaped signs hanging outside, and of course by irresistibly sugary, baking aromas wafting out into the street. In case those directions are too vague, try **Vanalinna Kohvik** (Suur-Karja 3) or **Otto Pagaripoisid** (Nunne 11). The town's oldest bakery/café, **Maiasmokk** (Pikk 16), is worth visiting for its old-fashioned decor, as well as its tempting cakes and handmade chocolates.

TRADITIONAL CUISINE

Sampling the local fare is a must when visiting Tallinn, but it's important to make the distinction between 'traditional Estonian cuisine' and what Estonians actually eat these days.

The former developed through centuries of Estonian village life, though it also shows clear Germanic and Scandinavian influences. Many of these dishes are, frankly, not for the faint hearted. One quintessentially Estonian item is *sült*, a jellied meat dish made by slowly reducing pork bones (and sometimes hooves and heads). It is served cold, with a touch of mustard or horseradish. Other traditional items include marinated eel, Baltic sprats and *mulgikapsad* (a kind of sauerkraut stew with pork). Pea soup with ham gets worked into the equation when the weather turns cold, and *verivorst* (blood sausage) is a Christmas favourite.

Pass the salt

'Our favourite spice is salt. When we're feeling really wild, we'll use a dash of pepper.'
– A local quip about the simplicity of Estonian cuisine.

Trying out these time-honoured dishes will definitely be an experience to remember, but these are only part of the story. Restaurants that specialise in Estonian cuisine always offer plenty of other,

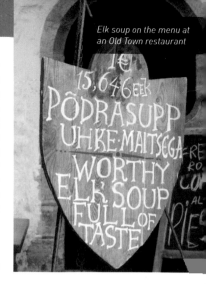
Elk soup on the menu at an Old Town restaurant

less daunting, choices for visitors who want to enjoy the traditional ambience without the jellied pork. A cosy place to try this food is the 1930s-style **Vanaema Juures** (Rataskaevu 10; tel: 6269 080), while the folksy **Kuldse Notsu Kõrts** (Dunkri 8; tel: 6286 567), places more emphasis on the sausages.

THE MODERN MENU

While nearly all Estonians will talk of traditional countryside food with patriotic, misty-eyed reverie, the truth is that hardly any of them will have it more than a couple of times a year, if at all. What locals are more likely to eat when they eat out is the simple, cheap and filling fare served in pubs and lunch cafés. Meals here typically consist of a piece of fried meat served with the obligatory side dish of boiled potatoes, a bit of cabbage or carrot, and a couple of slices of fresh tomato and cucumber. For the main item, *sealiha* (pork) is the definite favourite, with pork chops and pork *šnitsel* topping most menus. *Piprapihv* (pepper steak), *kanafilee* (chicken fillet), *grillitud forell* (grilled salmon), lamb and other basic meat dishes are also common.

Russian dishes such as *seljanka*, a meaty soup, and *pelmeenid*, a kind of ravioli served in a broth, are so widespread that many locals think of them as Estonian. Another favourite, particularly in summer, is *šašlõkk*, a shish kebab that comes from the Caucasus region.

Al fresco lunch on Viru Street

A much more recent trend in Estonia is the addition of exotic types of Baltic game to restaurant menus. A few establishments have started to serve elk, deer, bear and wild boar to curious carnivores. One Indian restaurant, **Elevant** (Vene 5; tel: 6313 132), even has a moose curry. Look for other versions of these unusual meats in restaurants around the Old Town.

WHEN ORDERING

Though it is mainly straightforward, the Estonian menu has a few nuances that can be confusing to foreigners. For instance, when ordering, it is important to keep in mind that a 'salad' may be a mixture of finely chopped meat, rice, potatoes or vegetables mixed with mayonnaise and served in a small dish. Anyone looking for a low-calorie plate of lettuce, carrots, olives and the like should consult the waiter for advice. A 'sandwich' in the local understanding is a single, small piece of bread topped with a simple piece of cheese, meat or fish.

Another twist is that pancakes, *pannkoogid*, are not primarily a breakfast food. Thick pancakes with savoury fillings such as ham and cheese, tuna, mushrooms and prawns are often served as a snack or a main lunch course, while honey- or jam-filled pancakes make popular desserts. Similarly, omelettes can just as easily be ordered for lunch or dinner as they can for breakfast.

After ordering, a basket of bread usually arrives at your table. The bread is always free, and its freshness is a good indicator of the quality of the food to come. Water, by contrast, does not typically come free as it does in many other countries, and has to be ordered by the glass or bottle.

SNACKS

Jäätis (ice cream) is the undisputed king of summertime snacks. Countless varieties are available from street vendors, shops and kiosks all over town. Other snacks include fresh strawberries, sometimes sold by teenagers milling through the Old Town, and roasted almonds covered in sugar and cinnamon that can be bought from an old-fashioned covered wagon.

⊘ VEGETARIAN OPTIONS

The idea of anyone willingly giving up meat is fairly baffling to the pork-chop-loving Estonians, so it is no surprise that Tallinn has no exclusively vegetarian restaurants. But vegetarians will not starve. Catering as they do to the international market, many restaurants in the Old Town have made one or two *taimetoidud* (vegetarian dishes) available. These range from fairly uninspired concoctions of stir-fried veggies or grilled cauliflower to very decent potato pancakes or stews. Note that salads and soups that would seem to be meat-free by their menu descriptions will often contain bits of ham. Consulting the waiter when ordering is the best way to avoid any surprises.

Ethnic restaurants, particularly Indian, Thai and Chinese, usually have the most promising vegetarian selections, often with a whole page of options. Italian restaurants will always have a pasta or pizza dish that is made without meat.

Almost as popular (but no more healthy) are the beer snacks served in restaurants and pubs. *Küüslauguleivad*, or garlic bread, which in the Estonian case is made of small, oily pieces of black bread, is the most popular of these. Another one to try, if your arteries can stand it, is *juustupallid*, or fried cheese balls.

DESSERT

Estonian restaurants always have plenty of *magustoidud* (desserts) to satisfy the most ravenous sweet tooth. *Pannkoogid* (pancakes) are highly popular and can be found on almost every menu. They come with a fruit, jam or honey filling, and can also be accompanied by the nation's other favourite, *jäätis* (ice cream). A truly unforgettable variation of ice cream that every visitor should try is the one with the city's famous Vana Tallinn liqueur (see page 91) dribbled over it.

Koogid (cakes) of various sorts are often available. The most typically Estonian (and delicious) of these are the ones made on a base of *kohupiim*, a kind of sweet cream cheese.

The time-honoured Estonian treat is *kama*, a thick mixture of grains and sour milk *(keefir)* that is served in the 'traditional' establishments. The curious will want to give it a try, but many foreigners find it simply too bizarre for their tastes.

⊘ THE ESTONIAN TOAST

Estonians aren't ones for long speeches; when they toast, they simply clink their glasses and say *'terviseks!'* ('to your health'). When going through this process though, it is absolutely vital to make eye-to-eye contact with each person as your glasses touch. Failure to do so is considered rude, and can lead to calls for you to repeat the toast the correct way.

DRINKS

When it comes to beverages, the nation's clear choice is beer (õlu). The unquestionable favourites among the Estonian brews are the two lagers, Saku Originaal and A. Le Coq Premium. One or the other can be found in almost every pub, café or restaurant. When trying other names, you may have to choose between a *hele* (light) or *tume* (dark) beer. Imports of popular international beers are also available, albeit at a higher price.

Coming in a close second to beer in popularity is Estonian vodka (viin). The Saaremaa Viin and Viru Valge brands are recommended. Wine (vein) has also been gaining popularity in recent years, particularly with the emergence of several elegant wine bars in the Old Town (see page 86).

Vana Tallinn, the city's signature liqueur, may look like something very old and traditional judging by its label, but it was invented in the 1960s as a kind of souvenir. Few locals drink the

Herring on dark bread – the Estonian national sandwich

sweet, dark liquid by itself. It works best when added to coffee or used to liven up a dessert.

In cold weather, there's no substitute for *hõõgvein*, a hot, spiced wine drink similar to Swedish *glögg*. A cup or two of *hõõgvein* at Christmas is enough to put anyone in the holiday spirit.

TO HELP YOU ORDER...

Could we have a table? **Palun kas me saaksime laua?**
I'd like a/an/some... **Ma sooviksin...**
The bill, please. **Palun arvet**

bread (dark) **leib**	fish **kala**
bread (light) **sai**	fruit **puuvili**
butter **või**	ice cream **jäätis**
coffee **kohv**	meat **liha**
dessert **dessert/**	menu **menüü**
magustoit	milk **piim**

pepper **pipar**
potatoes **kartulid**
rice **riis**
salad **salat**
salt **sool**
sandwich **võileib**

soup **supp**
sugar **suhkur**
tea **tee**
wine **vein**
vegetarian **taimetoitlane**
vodka **viin**

...AND READ THE MENU

eelroad starters
forell trout
hapukapsas sauerkraut
jäätis ice cream
juust cheese
kala fish
kalkun turkey
kana chicken
kartulid potatoes
kaste sauce
koha pike
kohv coffee
köögiviljad vegetables
koor cream
krevetid prawn
kurk cucumber
lasteroad children's
   menu
leib dark bread
liha meat
lisandid side orders
lõhe salmon
magustoi-dud desserts
õlu beer

omletid omelettes
pannkoogid pancakes
pardiliha duck
piim milk
porgand carrot
praed main
   courses
riis rice
sai white bread
salatid salads
sealiha pork
seened mushrooms
sink ham
supid soups
suupisted appetisers
taimetoi-dud vegetarian
   dishes
tee tea
tomat tomato
tuunikala tuna
vein wine
veiseliha beef
viin vodka
vesi water

PLACES TO EAT

The price categories below are based on the average cost of a three-course meal for one person, and do not include drinks or tip.

€€€€	over €35
€€€	€25–€35
€€	€15–€25
€	under €15

OLD TOWN

Beer House €€€ *Dunkri 5; tel: 644 2222; www.beerhouse.ee.* A lively venue on any given weekend, this vast, German-style beer hall is the place to go for hulking portions of meat and sausage. True to its name, it serves up seven varieties of house brew. Be sure to check out the inventive back 'courtyard' and be prepared for tourist-oriented Bavarian bands at night. Open daily noon–midnight.

Clayhills Gastropub €€€ *Pikk 13; tel: 6419 312; www.clayhills.ee.* Estonia's only gastropub is a relaxed destination for a quality meal, thanks to its cosy atmosphere and top-notch chef. It gets busier when sports are shown on TV or after 10pm at weekends, when the live jazz or guitar performances have started. Open daily noon–midnight.

Controvento €€ *Vene 12; tel: 6440 470; www.controvento.ee.* Consistently high-quality Italian cuisine and professional service has made Controvento a long-time favourite of Tallinn's expatriate community. The setting – a cosy medieval building in the Katariina passageway – encourages people to linger for hours, ordering course after course from *bruschetta* to *tiramisu*. Reservations at weekends are essential. Open daily noon–midnight.

Cru €€€€ *Viru 8; tel: 6140 085; www.crurestoran.eu.* Top-notch restaurant in the heart of Tallinn's Old Town. Cosy yet elegant, it offers a wide range of international dishes, including avocado steak for vegans and retro beefeater (roasted beef fillet with onion gravy and bone marrow), along with a range of fish and seafood dishes. Estonian haute cuisine at its best. Open daily noon–11pm.

Dominic €€€ *Vene 10; tel: 6410 400;* www.restoran.ee. A fine choice for a gourmet experience, Dominic serves up an inventive array of European-style dishes in its elegant rooms. More than that, this is a 'wine restaurant', and therefore an excellent place to enjoy one of the fine vintages carefully selected by the sommelier. Open Mon–Sat noon–midnight, Sun noon–9pm.

Elevant €€ *Vene 5; tel: 6313 132;* www.elevant.ee. One of the Old Town's finest Indian restaurants, Elevant could easily win awards with its interior design alone. Everything from the iron staircase to the beautifully furnished dining rooms makes this a soothing escape from the tourist bustle outside. A long list of traditional curries, biriyanis and masalas is rounded out with a clever, Estonian-inspired 'wild menu' that features items such as moose *vindaloo* and wild boar mushroom korma. Open daily noon–11pm.

Gloria €€€€ *Müürivahe 2; tel: 6406 800;* www.gloria.ee. Gloria is the sort of restaurant people go to when they truly want to spoil themselves. The restaurant, which opened in 1937, has hosted a number of statesmen and dignitaries, including Pope John Paul II and Lech Walesa. The interior is a study in pre-war decadence – antiques, potted palms and private booths closed off by velvet curtains. An interesting mix of French, Italian, Baltic and Russian creations makes up the menu. Anyone who wants to taste a bit of Gloria's glory without committing to a full meal can visit its attractive wine cellar. Open Mon–Sat 5.30–11.30pm.

Golden Dragon €€ *Pühavaimu 7; tel: 6313 506;* www.goldendragon.ee. This cellar venue might look tired compared to the rash of flashier Chinese restaurants that have opened since the end of the 1990s, but Golden Dragon wins the race because of its consistently scrumptious food and great service. It can also be economical – portions of spring rolls are large enough to share, and the lunch special (served Mon–Fri noon–4pm) includes rice, soup, salad and main course for just €5. Open daily noon–11pm.

Kaerajaan €€€ *Raekoja plats 17; tel: 6155 400; www.kaerajaan.ee.* For an inventive spin on Estonian ingredients – and folk patterns – head to this bright restaurant overlooking Town Hall Square. Both the colourful ground-floor café and the more formal upper floors display fun-loving décor. The food, while not resembling anything traditionally Estonian, will more than satisfy. Open daily 10am–midnight.

Kompressor € *Rataskaevu 3; tel: 6464 210; www.kompressorpub.ee.* More of a pub than a fully-fledged restaurant, this popular student haunt is a budget traveller's dream. There are other items on the menu, but what draws the crowds to Kompressor are its enormous pancakes filled with things like smoked chicken, turkey, prawns and garlic cheese. One portion is a meal in itself and, at around €5, a true bargain. Be prepared to wait. Open daily 11am–11pm.

Le Bonaparte €€€ *Pikk 45; tel: 6464 444; www.bonaparte.ee.* Enjoy fine, French cuisine in a beautifully restored, 17th-century merchant's house. Guests can opt for the formal dining in the main restaurant or the cosier cellar downstairs, or just drop into the foyer café for pastries and cakes. In all cases, it's a quality experience. Open Sun–Thu 11am–10pm, Fri–Sat 11am–1am.

Lusikas €€–€€€ *Aia 7; tel: 6463 030; http://restoranlusikas.ee.* Slightly off the beaten path, this relatively young restaurant specialises in French cuisine, with items like veal blanquette and leg of rabbit on the menu. Highly professional staff treat the customers with care in the sophisticated, modern dining room. Open Mon–Sat noon–11pm, Sun until 9pm.

Must Puudel €–€€ *Müürivahe 20; tel: 5056 258.* A trip back in time to the Soviet 1980s – thankfully extending only to the interior decor – has made the Black Poodle a favourite among young locals, many of whom crowd in late at night for wine and laughs. Genuine, junky remnants of the era have been cleverly arranged to create a casual atmosphere that is rounded out by quite decent, inexpensive food and cheerful service. Open Sun–Tue 9am–11pm, Wed 9am–1am, Thur–Sat 9am–2am.

Olde Hansa €€€ *Vana turg 1; tel: 6279 020;* www.oldehansa.ee. This medieval-style restaurant in the heart of the Old Town may appear touristy from the outside, but once you dine here you will understand why a visit to Tallinn would not be complete without experiencing Olde Hansa. Far more intricate and authentic than a typical theme restaurant, it offers a fascinating menu and a truly Hanseatic atmosphere, complete with costumed waitresses, candlelight and minstrels. Reserve at weekends. Open daily 11am–midnight.

Peppersack €€€ *Viru 2/Vana turg 6; tel: 6466 800;* www.peppersack.ee. Not quite the medieval experience one might expect when looking from the outside, Peppersack is nevertheless worth a visit for its beautiful, historic interior, friendly service and good food. With the tourist very much in mind, it stages a sword fight drama every evening, as well as belly dance performances on Fridays and Saturdays. Open Mon–Sat 8am–midnight, Sun 9–11pm.

Ribe €€€ *Vene 7; tel: 6313 084;* www.ribe.ee. Ribe was founded by three of Estonia's top waiters, and it delivers a gourmet dining experience that few others are able to match. With its tasteful, Nordic decor, it is an excellent representation of the direction that the nation's dining scene is heading. Open Mon 5–11pm, Tue–Fri noon–3pm and 5–11pm, Sat noon–11pm.

Silk €€€ *Kullassepa 4; tel: 6659 309;* www.silk.ee. A long list of intriguing sushi choices, soups, tempura and other Japanese favourites are on the menu at Silk. The black interior gives this small restaurant a chic, cosmopolitan feel and the location near Town Hall Square makes it equally popular. For something different, try the green-tea-flavoured ice cream. Open daily 10am–9pm.

Tchaikovsky €€€ *Vene 9 (Hotel Telegraaf); tel: 6000 610;* www.telegraaf hotel.com/et/restoran-tallinnas. Advertised as a 'symphony of Russian cuisine', this is one of Estonia's top restaurants. Blending French tastes, Russian traditions and Estonian ingredients, it has an opulent 19th-century interior and a classy menu featuring such delicacies as bluefin tuna tartar, pigeon royal, and roasted cod or venison. Menu degustation 6 (at

€80 per person) is probably the least economically painful option. Open Mon–Fri 12.30–3pm and 6–11pm, Sat–Sun 1–11pm.

Troika €€ *Raekoja plats 15; tel: 6276 245;* www.troika.ee. Resembling something straight out of a 19th-century Russian storybook, this lavishly decorated cellar restaurant is not one you will soon forget. The menu ranges from blini to Tver mutton and includes bear stroganoff. The Town Hall Square location makes Troika a busy place, so reserve a table. Open daily 11am–11pm.

Vanaema Juures €€ *Rataskaevu 10/12; tel: 6269 080;* www.vonkrahl. ee. Just as you might expect from a restaurant called Grandmother's Place, this quiet cellar venue is bursting with antiques and old photographs and has a friendly atmosphere. It is also Tallinn's cosiest Estonian restaurant and an excellent place to try national dishes. Open daily noon–10pm.

Von Krahli Aed €€ *Rataskaevu 8; tel: 5859 3839;* www.vonkrahl.ee. A tasteful, earthy interior, cosy ambience and consistently excellent food at bargain prices have made Aed one of the most popular of Tallinn's dining establishments, so reservations are highly recommended. The menu focuses on fresh, natural ingredients and features more vegetarian options than most. Open Mon–Sat noon–midnight, Sun noon–11pm.

KALAMAJA

Boheem € *Kopli 18; tel: 6311 928;* www.boheem.ee. The laid-back, Bohemian spirit of the Kalamaja neighbourhood is typified by this pleasant café, which is often packed by student types in eyeglasses and scarves. Light meals like salads, pancakes and wraps are available at extremely reasonable prices. Open Mon–Fri 9am–11pm, Sat–Sun 10am–11pm.

F-Hoone € *Telliskivi 60a; tel: 5322 6855.* Well off the beaten path and cleverly built into a former factory space, F-Hoone displays the kind of edginess that the latest generation of Tallinners has come to love. It operates as a restaurant by day, serving inexpensive meals, and turns into a bar and club on weekend nights. Find it by crossing to the back of the train station, heading east down Kopli and turning left at the first tram stop. Open Mon–Sat 9am–midnight, Sun 9am–10pm.

CITY CENTRE AND KADRIORG

Alter Ego €€ *Roseni 8; tel: 54 56 0339;* www.alterego.ee. With its airy interior, crisp service and relaxed feel, Alter Ego exudes the spirit of the Rotermann Quarter, where it makes its home. It is Spanish owned, and the menu is a mix of Mediterranean and Estonian-based choices. Freshly baked bread, and sorbets and ice creams made in-house round out the top-quality offerings. Open daily 11.00am–11pm.

Lido € *Estonia pst. 9; tel: 6093 364;* www.lido.ee. Located on the second floor of the Solaris Centre, the local branch of Latvia's favourite chain restaurant is a great choice for travellers on a budget. Wide selections of salads, mains, garnishes and desserts are freshly prepared and served up buffet/cafeteria style, then enjoyed in a vast, busy dining hall that resembles a fairy-tale village. Open daily 10am–10pm.

NOP € *Köleri 1; tel: 6032 270;* http://blog.nop.ee. For young locals and savvy expats, a stop at this earthy little café is a must when in the Kadriorg area. Natural and health foods dominate the chalkboard menu, which mostly offers pastries, sandwiches and other light dishes. Those looking for something truly different should try one of the fruit smoothies. Open Mon–Fri 8am–9pm, weekends 9am–9pm.

Ö €€€€ *Mere pst. 6E; tel: 6616 150;* www.restoran-o.ee. Local gourmands habitually praise this ultra-stylish establishment that sits between Old Town and the Passenger Port. Both the chef and the restaurant itself have won multiple culinary awards through the years thanks to unsurpassed cuisine and an elegant dining environment. Expect a creative, international menu. Open Wed–Sat 6–11pm.

Platz €€–€€€ *Roseni 7; tel: 6645 086;* www.platz.ee. This cosy, brick-lined restaurant at the heart of the Rotermann Quarter has become known for consistently serving up great contemporary cuisine. The menu is short, but what the kitchen staff prepare, they prepare well and specials change day by day depending on whatever interesting ingredients become available. Open Mon–Sat noon–11pm, Sun until 10pm.

Rataskaevu 16 €€ *16 Rataskaevu; tel: 642 4025;* http://rataskaevu16.ee. Tallin's top-rated restaurant attracts its fair share of local and international gourmets who come here to taste the best Estonian food including famous fried herring fillets or elk roast. Vegetarians will also find plenty of options here. In summer, choose a table on the wonderful patio. Open Mon–Thu and Sun noon–11pm, Fri–Sat until midnight.

Restoran Kadriorg €€€ *Weizenbergi 18; tel: 6013 636.* Catering to the demands of Kadriorg's young, professional elite, this relatively new restaurant is a modern and trendy alternative to typically traditional upmarket fare. One floor offers a short, European menu heavy on grill items, while another is a 'spaghetteria', where pasta is king. Open Mon–Sat noon–11pm, Sun 3–10pm.

Tar Tar Bar €€ *Narva mnt. 7; tel: 6109 230.* One of the trendier restaurants that has cropped up in recent years in the business district of the capital. Modern European cuisine and Estonian staples, such as selyanka (a hearty, smoky meat soup), are served in a sleek, copper-toned bar. Lunch on weekdays is excellent value. Open Mon–Thu noon–10pm, Fri–Sat noon–1am.

Villa Thai €€ *Vilmsi 6; tel: 6419 347;* www.villathai.ee. Spicy Thai delicacies and irresistible Indian (tandoori) specialities are equally available at this popular Kadriorg haunt. The management takes extra care to ensure a soothing ambience, Buddha statue and indoor fountain included. Lunch specials are also available, served weekdays, noon–3pm. Open Mon–Sat noon–11pm, Sun 2–11pm.

A-Z TRAVEL TIPS

A SUMMARY OF PRACTICAL INFORMATION

A

ACCOMMODATION

Hotels in the centre of Tallinn historically came in two varieties: small, stylish, exclusive establishments within the Old Town, and large, towering, chain-type hotels just outside the Old Town. These are now being joined by large spa hotels and mid-range options in the city centre. Prices can vary substantially, so comparison-shopping is always a good idea. Many hotels offer discounts of 5–15 percent to customers booking online. Bargain hunters should also note that rates for equivalent hotels located a short distance from the centre can be substantially lower.

For travellers staying three days or more, renting a serviced flat is an alternative worth considering. Prices per night become cheaper the longer you stay.

Family-run guesthouses and a few Soviet-era dormitories that have been turned into hotels provide cheap accommodation on Tallinn's periphery. For apartment rentals, check www.apartment.ee.

In all cases, booking well in advance is recommended. The best resource for accommodation information is the Tallinn Tourism Office's extensive website (www.visittallinn.ee).

> I've a reservation. **Mul on tuba broneeritud.**
> I'd like a single/double room with a bath/shower. **Ma sooviksin ühelist/kahelist tuba vanniga/duššiga.**

AIRPORT

The **Lennart Meri Tallinn Airport** (TLL; www.tallinn-airport.ee) is incredibly close to the city centre, making it a convenient gateway to Estonia's capital.

Arrival and departure areas are located in two halves of the same long hall. As you enter the arrival area after baggage claim, ATMs and banks are to your left, towards the centre of the hall. An information desk just beyond them only provides details on the airport itself and how to get into town. Car-hire companies are downstairs.

Taxis wait just outside the arrivals area's main door, straight ahead. An airport transfer by taxi can take as little as 10 minutes and the fare should be under €10. Bus stops are located on the lower concourse, one escalator flight down from the arrivals hall. Buses to the centre depart from stop No. 1. City bus No. 2, which will take you to a stop next to the Viru shopping mall in the centre, departs from the airport every 20–30 minutes. Its timetable is posted next to the stop. The 10-minute journey costs €2. Pay the driver as you board. You can also take tram route 4 (5.30am–12.45am) which takes you to the city centre in just 15–17 minutes.

> What bus do I take to the centre? **Missugune buss sôidab kesklinna?**
> How much is the fare to ...? **Kui palju maksab pilet ...?**
> Will you tell me when to get off? **Palun öelge kus ma pean väljuma?**

B

BICYCLE HIRE

Getting around by bicycle is a perfect way to explore the leafy Kadriorg district, the Pirita beach area and the shoreline that stretches between them.

City Bike (Vene tn. 33; tel: 5111 819; www.citybike.ee) hires out bikes for periods ranging from one to three hours (€7) to five or more days (€9 per day). The price includes safety equipment and locks. The firm can deliver and pick up bicycles from other locations.

BUDGETING FOR YOUR TRIP

Prices in Tallinn are generally cheaper than in other European capitals, particularly for food and drink. Those planning to do extensive sight-seeing should consider picking up the city's discount card, the **Tallinn Card**, available in 24-, 48- and 72-hour versions at €25, €37 and €45, respectively. The card gives holders free access to more than 40 top of the city's attractions and museums, free use of public transport (plus hop-on hop-off buses) and discounts in a number of shops and restaurants, as well as reduced prices of sightseeing tours. Consider carefully before buying one on a Monday or Tuesday, when many museums are closed. Cards are sold at the Tourist Information Centres (see page 130) and at larger hotels.

Accommodation. Youth hostel travellers can find beds for about €10, though most are in the €10–€15 range. A budget hotel with an en-suite will be €40–€70, whereas high-end establishments will charge €90 and up.

Buses and trams. Single-ride tickets purchased from the driver cost €2, a 1-hour E-Ticket (Smartcard) validation costs €1.10 and an all-day ticket costs €3. A smartcard, which can be bought at any R-Kiosk, post office or government office, can be used for a group of up to six people.

Entertainment. Mid-range tickets to a symphony concert average €20, cinema tickets at weekends cost €7.50, and entrance to a popular nightclub costs €10 to €12.

Food and drink. A light lunch, without drinks, can be had for between €8 and €10 per person, whereas an average three-course evening meal will run to €20 or €30. A large beer in a local pub costs €3.50, and in a touristy café, €5. Soft drinks are usually priced at about €1.50.

Museums. Museum tickets for adults usually cost between €4 and €8.

C

CAR HIRE

Unless you plan to travel around the countryside during your stay, there's no real need to hire a car when visiting Tallinn. Nearly all the important sites are within easy walking distance of one another; the rest can be reached with a short tram or bus ride.

Most of the major international car-hire agencies operate in the city. All have rental desks on the lower floor of Tallinn Airport, and some also have offices in the city centre.

To hire a car, a driver must be at least 21 years of age, possess a valid driving licence with photo, and must have held a licence for at least two years.

Avis: at the airport, tel: 6058 222; in the city at Järvevana tee 9, tel: 6671 500; www.avis.ee.

Budget: at the airport, tel: 6058 600; www.budget.ee.

Hertz: at the airport, tel. 6058 923; in the city at Ahtri 12, tel: 6116 333; www.hertz.ee.

R-Rent: at the airport, tel: 5036 446; www.rrent.ee.

Sir Rent: Tatari 56 , tel: 5651 353; www.sirrent.ee.

Sixt: at the airport, tel: 6058 142; in the city at Rävala 5; www.sixt.ee.

> I'd like to hire a car. **Ma sooviksin üürida autot.**
> I'd like it for a day/week. **Ma sooviksin seda üheks päevaks nädalaks.**
> Where's the nearest petrol station? **Kus on lähim bensiinijaam?**

CLIMATE

Winter days can be either bitterly cold or uncomfortably damp. Spring and autumn are unpredictable, with temperatures hovering just above freezing. The best time to visit is unquestionably summer, when the weather is mildest and the northern skies stay light until after 11pm, although June and July are also the wettest months, and can bring heavy rain showers. The following chart shows the average monthly highs and lows in Tallinn:

	J	F	M	A	M	J	J	A	S	O	N	D
°C	0	-1	2	9	13	19	22	20	15	10	3	0
	5	-7	-5	0	3	9	11	10	6	3	-1	-5
°F	32	29	36	49	56	66	71	69	60	50	38	31
	22	17	22	32	38	48	53	51	43	38	29	22

CLOTHING

Light, summer attire is perfect for touring the city in the high season, but keep in mind that warm, sunny days can quickly turn cool, so it is always a good idea to carry along an extra layer of clothing. A light, waterproof jacket will also come in handy. Anyone visiting Tallinn in winter should pack heavy coats, scarves, gloves, boots – and a sense of humour. For touring the uneven, cobbled streets of the Old Town, sturdy shoes are a must.

Smart dress is the norm for diners in moderate to expensive restaurants. The same is true of nightclubs.

CRIME AND SAFETY

Your chances of becoming the victim of a crime are remote, but the city is not crime-free. The most common offences against foreigners involve mugging and petty theft, an activity that is concentrated in the Old Town, on Viru Street in particular. Take care that your wallet isn't temptingly jutting from your pocket, and that your bag, camera or mobile phone is not sitting too close to the outer rail of the café. Leave valuables in your hotel, preferably in the safe, and keep your car in a guarded car park at night.

Violent crime against foreigners is rare, but you can use common sense to reduce the risk. Avoid unfamiliar, unlit areas at night, particularly if you are alone. Drink responsibly, and don't end up stumbling out of a pub late at night with a group of strangers. If you fall victim to a crime, call the general emergency number: 112 or the Tallinn Central Police Station (tel: 6125 400).

Call the police. **Kutsuge politsei.**
My handbag/wallet has been stolen. **Minu käekoti/rahakoti
   on ära varastatud.**
Stop thief! **Peatage varas!**
Help! **Appi!**
Leave me alone! **Jätke mind rahule!**

D

DRIVING

Road conditions. Road conditions in Estonia are generally good, both in Tallinn and on motorways. The biggest hazard is usually other drivers, whose habits range from the careless to the aggressive. Your only recourse is to drive defensively. Weather is the next issue, particularly in winter when patches of ice appear on streets and roads. If you don't know how to drive in winter conditions, this is not the place to learn. Also, because markings on rural routes can often be confusing, a good road atlas is essential. Finally, drivers unfamiliar with Tallinn should avoid the Old Town, with its confusing system of one-way streets.

Road signs. Traffic signs and symbols in Estonia follow the European standard.

Rules and regulations. Drive on the right and overtake on the left. Estonian law requires that headlights be kept on at all times, day and night, even in the city. The basic speed limit outside built-up areas is 90km/h (56mph), in built-up areas 50km/h (31mph), and in residential areas 20km/h (13mph). Some roads are marked with their own limits, particularly large motorways, where cars are permitted to travel at 110km/h (69mph) in summer. In the city, passengers in both front seats must wear seatbelts at all times. On motorways, the same rule applies to back-seat passengers as well. Children under 12 are not allowed in the front seat. Winter tyres must be used from 1 December to

1 March, though the dates can change from year to year. Valid foreign driving licences can be used in Estonia for up to a year; no international licence is needed.

Filling up. First pump, then pay. Fuel comes in four varieties: 92, 95, 98 and diesel. Most drivers use the 95 or the higher-quality 98. A litre of fuel generally costs around €1.26.

Parking. Finding street parking in Tallinn's busy centre can be a true test of will. Most is paid parking, but the first 15 minutes is free (except in private car parks). Tickets are sold in vending machines or via mobile applications for between €0.60 and €6 per hour, depending on the area. Car parks/garages may be an easier option in central Tallinn. These can be found under Freedom Square (Vabaduse väljak), on Rävala 5, and in the Viru Centre (Viru Väljak 4/6). The cost is typically €2 per hour. For details on parking in Tallinn, consult the excellent website www.parkimine.ee.

If you need help. Dial 118 for road service. They will tow your car to the nearest garage. If you need police or an ambulance, dial 112.

Are we on the right road for ...? **Kas me oleme õigel teel ...?**
Fill the tank, please with 92/95/98/diesel. **Palun täitke paak 92/95/98/diisel.**
My car has broken down. **Mu auto läks katki.**
There's been an accident. **Juhtus õnnetus.**

E

ELECTRICITY

The electricity in Estonia is 220 volts AC, 50Hz. Plugs are the round, two-pinned variety used in continental Europe, and adaptors can be found in electronic shops and in department stores.

EMBASSIES AND CONSULATES

Note that some embassies that serve Estonia are not in Estonia.

Australia. Klarabergsviadukten 63, 8th fl. 111 64 Stockholm, Sweden; tel: (+46 8) 613 29 00; www.sweden.embassy.gov.au.

Canada. Toomkooli 13, Tallinn; tel: 6273 311; www.estonia.gc.ca.

Ireland. Rahukohtu 4-II, Tallinn; tel: 6811 870; www.embassyofireland.ee.

South Africa. Pohjoinen Makasiinikatu 4, Helsinki, Finland; tel: (+358 9) 686 03 100; www.dirco.gov.za/helsinki.

UK. Wismari 6, Tallinn; tel: 6674 700; www.gov.uk/world/organisations/british-embassy-tallinn.

US. Kentmanni 20, Tallinn; tel: 6688 100; https://ee.usembassy.gov.

> Where is the British/American Embassy? **Kus on Inglise/Ameerika saatkond?**

EMERGENCIES

Police, fire, paramedics: 112

> Where can I find a doctor who speaks English? **Kust ma võiksin leida arsti, kes räägib inglise keelt?**

> **G**

GETTING TO TALLINN

From the UK. British Airways (www.britishairways.com) and the budget airlines Easyjet (www.easyjet.com; flying from Gatwick) and Ryanair (www.ryanair.com; flying from Stansted) all operate direct flights between London and Tallinn, as does the Latvian low-cost airline airBaltic (www.airbaltic.com; flying from Gatwick). Other airlines, such as SAS (www.scandinavian.net) and Finnair (www.finnair.com), offer flights that connect through Copenhagen and Helsinki respectively, though these routes are usually more expensive.

From outside Europe. There are two basic strategies: get the best deal you can on a flight to London, then take an Easyjet, Ryanair or airBaltic flight (*see above*), or use one of the airlines that can connect you to Tallinn through its regional hub. The major airlines with services to Tallinn are airBaltic, Finnair, SAS, Lufthansa and LOT Polish Airways.

From neighbouring countries. If you are travelling from elsewhere in the Baltics or Central Europe, the bus, not the train, is the way to go. Eurolines (www.eurolines.com) offers frequent connections and good rates. From the north, overnight ferries make a slow connection from Stockholm, and each day dozens of ships make the quick, 85km (53-mile) crossing from Helsinki.

GUIDES AND TOURS

A wide range of intriguing city tours is available, from self-guided audio-tours to offbeat, themed group tours. Tourist Information (see page 130) provides a complete list and can also put you in touch with a private guide. Among the more popular tours is the **Hop-on Hop-Off City Tour** (tel: 5301 5623; www.citytour.ee), which operates open-top buses on three regular routes. For a well-rounded, standard orientation, try the **Tallinn Official Sightseeing Tour** operated by Reisiekspert (tel: 6108 616; https://travel-expert.eu). The combina-

Is there an English-speaking guide? **Kas teil on inglise keelt kõnelev giid?**
Can you translate this for me? **Kas te oskate seda mulle tõlkida?**

tion bus and walking tour covers all the city's major sights Another option is the **Welcome to Tallinn bicycle tour** organised by City Bike (tel: 5111 819; www.citybike.ee). The same company offers a Soviet-themed bike tour and a walking tour. The more adventurous can try the **Sea Kayak Tour** run by 360 (tel: 5686 4634; www.360.ee), which lets visitors paddle out into the bay for a different view of the medieval skyline. No experience is required. Meanwhile **Tallinn Traveller** (tel: 5837 4800; www.traveller.ee) offers several walking and bike tours, as well as daily trips from Tallinn.

H

HEALTH AND MEDICAL CARE

Visiting Estonia poses no significant health risks and there are no issues with water quality. One concern however, which only applies to visitors who spend time deep in the Estonian wilderness, is tick-borne encephalitis. If you plan to explore a forested area, you should get a vaccination before leaving home.

Western-produced medicines, including many of the same brands you would find at home, are widely available from any pharmacy (apteek). Staff in central locations generally speak English, but selection is limited, so if you need a very specialised product, it is best to

---

Where's the nearest (all-night) pharmacy? **Kus on lähim (ööpäev lahti olev) apteek?**
I need a doctor/dentist. **Ma vajan arsti/hambaarsti.**
an ambulance **kiirabi**
hospital **haigla**
an upset stomach **kõht on korrast ära**
I have a stomach ache/ sunburn/a fever. **Minu kõht valutab/päikesepõletus/palavik.**

bring it with you. The **Tõnismäe Apteek** (Tõnismägi 5; tel: 6442 282) runs an all-night pharmacy window.

Estonia's healthcare system provides free emergency assistance to all visitors, and those who hold the European Health Insurance Card (EHIC) are entitled to the same services as locals. However, it is still advisable to arrange a travel insurance policy that includes medical care before your trip.

The state-run hospitals in Estonia are hit-and-miss in terms of service, and most foreigners use them only if absolutely necessary. The standards at private clinics are much better, but these generally don't provide emergency services. If you have a medical problem, you can contact Tallinn's **Central Hospital** (Keskhaigla; Ravi 18; tel: 6661 900; www.itk.ee). If an ambulance is needed, call 112.

L

LANGUAGE

The national language is Estonian, a Finno-Ugric tongue related to Finnish and Hungarian, but completely unrecognisable to Estonia's other neighbours. Its complicated grammatical structure and baffling vowels have given it the reputation of being one of the world's most difficult languages to learn. Fortunately, English is widely spoken in the capital, and you should have no trouble communicating.

Do you speak English? **Kas te räägite inglise keelt?**
Hello **Tere**
Goodbye **Head aega/nägemist**
Pardon me **Vabandust**
Please **Palun**
Thank you **Aitäh**
Cheers! **Terviseks!**

LGBTQ TRAVELLERS

Though the situation is improving, attitudes towards homosexuality in Estonia have not caught up with those in other European countries. Overt displays, such as holding hands, may attract the wrong sort of attention. Local-life.com/tallinn offers tips and advice to LGBTQ travellers and lists the city's handful of gay bars and clubs. X-Baar (Tatari 1; www.xbaar.ee/en) is the most established of these, but Club 69 (Sakala 24; www.club69.ee), a bar and sauna, is at least as popular.

M

MAPS

Free maps are available at the Tourist Information Centre (see page 130). Additionally, all the free tourist/shopping guides floating around Tallinn will have a map of the Old Town you can tear out. More detailed local and regional maps, such as the one published by Regio, can be found in the Rahva Raamat bookshop (www.rahvaraamat.ee) on the 3rd floor of the Viru shopping centre, Viru väljak 4/6.

MEDIA

Press. A handful of English-language city guides can be found in town, but the best of the bunch is the invaluable *Tallinn In Your Pocket*. The region's only English-language newspaper is the Riga-based weekly *The Baltic Times* (www.baltictimes.com). International newspapers can be found in major hotels and larger downtown kiosks.

Radio. Raadio Tallinn (103.5MHz FM; https://raadiotallinn.err.ee) re-broadcasts the BBC World Service daily. Pop music stations include Sky Plus (92.6MHz) and Power Hit Radio (102.1MHz).

Television. Estonia's three major broadcasters are the public Estonian National Broadcasting (ETV, ETV2, ETV+), the commercial Kanal2, which also runs channels 11 and 12, and TV3, which also runs its entertainment-style programmes on TV6. All have a number of imported shows in English.

MONEY

Estonia uses the euro (EUR). Banknotes come in denominations of 500, 200, 100, 50, 20, 10 and 5 euros, and coins in denominations of 2 and 1 euros, and 50, 20, 10, 5, 2 and 1 cents.

Currency exchange. A number of colourful, brightly lit currency exchanges dot Old Town but almost always offer fantastically bad rates. You will get a much better deal from any commercial bank such as Swedbank, SEB or Nordea. Otherwise Tavid (Aia 5) operates a 24-hour exchange window that will do in a necessity.

ATMs. These are never hard to come by in Tallinn, especially in the touristy Old Town.

Traveller's cheques. Traveller's cheques from major issuers such as Thomas Cook and American Express are exchangeable at most banks, but are not accepted as payment in shops, restaurants or hotels.

Can I pay with this credit card? **Kas ma saan selle kreeditkaardiga maksta?**

I want to change some pounds/dollars. **Ma soovin vahetada naelasid/dollareid.**

Can you cash a traveller's cheque? **Kas te saaksite reisitšekke rahaks vahetada?**

Where's the nearest bank/ currency exchange office? **Kus on lähim pank/valuutavahetus?**

Is there a cash machine near here? **Kas lähedal on pangaautomaat?**

How much is that? **Kui palju see maksab?**

O

OPENING TIMES

Opening hours vary from business to business, but most follow these general customs:

Banks are open 9am–6pm Monday to Friday, with some of the larger branches open 10am–3pm on Saturday.

Museums are open 10am–6pm. Most are closed Monday or Tuesday.

Small shops open at 10am and close 5–7pm Monday to Friday. Some are closed Saturdays, but most open 10am–3 or 4pm. They are almost always closed Sundays. **Department stores** and **shopping centres**, on the other hand, stay open much later. These are open 9am–9pm daily, sometimes closing an hour or two earlier on Sundays.

Restaurants generally open at 11am or noon and close at 11pm or midnight. Some stay open one or two hours later on Friday and Saturday nights. Sundays are slow for restaurants, prompting a few to close their doors at 6pm. At weekends, the popular **bars** and **pubs** in the Old Town stay open until 3 or 4am.

P

POLICE

Estonia's national **Politsei**, seen roving the streets in dark-blue jumpsuits, are responsible for stopping crime and keeping order. Those assigned to the Old Town usually understand at least some English or will call a colleague who can. The green-clad **Munitsipaalpolitsei**, or municipal police, mainly issue fines for riding buses without tickets or violating city ordinances. If you find yourself in need of the police, call 112, or report crimes at the main police station at Kolde pst. 65; tel: 6125 400.

Where's the nearest police station? **Kus on lähim politseijaoskond?**
I've lost my wallet/bag/passport **Kaotasin oma rahakoti/koti/passi.**

POST OFFICE

Postal services are handled by Eesti Post (www.post.ee). For any postal services, Tallinn's Central Post Office *(postkontor)*, located at Narva mnt. 1 across from the Viru Hotel, should be your first stop. It is open 8am–8pm Monday to Friday, 10am–4pm Saturday, and English-speakers are plentiful. Letters and faxes are sent from the main hall upstairs, and packages from a ground-floor office on the left side of the building.

Stamps are also sold in most kiosks and by many of the postcard vendors operating stands in Old Town. Drop your postcards and letters in any of the bright, orange post boxes you see around town, or in the old-fashioned, green boxes in Old Town. Both are decorated with Eesti Post's bugle symbol.

> Where's the nearest post office? **Kus on lähim postkontor?**
> express (special delivery) **kullerteenus registered**

PUBLIC HOLIDAYS

The following are public holidays in Estonia when banks, shops and offices are closed. Restaurants, cafés and bars usually close only on Christmas, New Year's Day and Midsummer.

New Year's Day 1 January
Independence Day (1918) 24 February
Good Friday and Easter March or April
Spring Day 1 May
Whitsunday 20 May
Victory Day 23 June
Midsummer Day (St John's Day) 24 June
Day of Restoration of Independence 20 August
Christmas 25 December
Boxing Day 26 December

T

TELEPHONES

To phone Estonia from abroad, dial your international access code (00 in the UK), Estonia's country code (372), and then the number as listed. There are no city codes to add or digits to drop.

When phoning abroad from Estonia, dial 00, then your country code. If you need information or assistance from an operator, or you want to connect to an operator in your own country, dial 1184. Direct access numbers to organisations like AT&T will allow you to make credit-card calls or, in some cases, to reverse the charges (call collect). AT&T: 80 012 001; MCI 80 012 122; Canadian Teleglobe 80 012 011; BT 80 010 442.

Roaming is possible with any mobile phone that uses the standard European band. To avoid roaming charges, you can invest in a local SIM card, available from most kiosks. The starter kits, sold under brand names such as Telia or Elisa, cost €3–€5.

Public telephones have been phased out.

TIME ZONES

Estonia is in the Eastern European Time Zone. As in the UK, Daylight Saving Time is in effect from the last Sunday in March to the last Sunday in October. The following chart shows the time in various cities in summer.

San Francisco	New York	London	**Tallinn**	Sydney
2am	5am	10am	**noon**	7pm

TIPPING

Tipping in Estonia is somewhat haphazard. Some people tip, some do not. In restaurants you can reward good service with a 10 percent tip, and it is best to do so in cash. Tips will not be expected for meals in simpler cafés, pubs, or anywhere you pay at the till. Taxi drivers do not get tips, but you can round up to the next euro. Hotel porters should get around €2, and tour guides for large groups are usually tipped €1–€2 by each person.

TOILETS

In Estonia the WC *(veetsee)* is sometimes marked using a baffling system of triangles. A triangle pointing downwards is the men's room (think of a man with large shoulders), and one pointing up is the women's (think of a dress). Otherwise, men's and women's are marked *Meeste* (M) and *Naiste* (N) respectively. Public toilets, some of which are in the form of coin-operated kiosks, usually cost 20 cents If out and about in Old Town, you can find public toilets near the Viru Gates on Valli, in the underground walkway beneath Freedom Square and on Toompea next to the Aleksander Nevsky Cathedral.

Where are the toilets? **Kus on WC (veetsee)?**

TOURIST INFORMATION

The best place to find in-depth, authoritative information is the Tallinn Tourist Information Centre in the heart of the Old Town at Niguliste 2/Kullassepa 4 (Jan–Mar Mon–Sat 9am–7pm, Sun 10am–3pm; Apr–May and Sept Mon–Sat 9am–6pm, Sun 9am–4pm; Jun–Aug Mon–Sat 9am–7pm, Sun 9am–6pm; Oct–Dec Mon–Sat 9am–5pm, Sun 10am–3pm; tel: 6457 777; www.visittallinn.ee).

The Estonian Tourism Board provides general travel information about the country on its website, www.visitestonia.com.

TRANSPORT

City transit. The united system of buses, trams and electric trolleybuses that makes up Tallinn's public transport system operates in general from 6am to 11pm. It is run by the TLT Company, whose website (www.tallinnlt.ee) displays timetables, maps and a route planner in English. Maps posted on most bus stops will also show you how to make your journey, and you can call tel: 6434 142 during working hours for further info. Trams mainly service the centre of town, whereas the buses and trolleybuses will take you to outlying areas. Single-ride tickets can be bought from the driver for €2, but the most common way to pay is by E-Ticket (Smartcard), an electronic card sold and reloaded in post offices and kiosks in varying denominations. There is a €2 fee for new cards. Board from any door and validate your ticket by touching one of the round validators with it. Each validation costs €1.10 and is good for one hour. In any given 24-hour period you will never be charged more than the daily pass rate of €3. The system also works with contactless bank cards. Holders of the Tallinn Card, which is available from the Tourist Information Office (see page 130) and larger hotels, are entitled to unlimited free use of public transport (see page 116), and should validate their rides in the same manner.

Inter-city buses. Tallinn's bus station (Bussijaam; Lastekodu 46; tel: 12550; www.tpilet.ee) is just outside the city centre and can be reached by trams No. 2 and 4. Its website lists all times and prices in English. Buses to St Petersburg, Riga and other international destinations are operated by Lux Express (www.luxexpress.eu), which has a separate office in the bus station.

Taxis. The biggest complaint among tourists is taxi drivers who overcharge. By law, all taxis are required to clearly state their rates, in English, on large yellow stickers on their right passenger windows. But there is no law saying that these rates cannot be exorbitant. Normal rates consist of a base fare of max €5.50 plus a per-kilometre charge of max €1.10. Be wary of anyone asking for more. You can order a taxi by phone for the same price as getting one on the street. A good, cheap company is Reval Takso (tel: 1207; www.reval-takso.

ee). Controllers at the pricier Tulika Takso (tel: 1200; http://tulika.ee) might speak better English.

Where can I get a taxi? **Kust ma saaksin takso?**
What's the fare to (the centre)? **Palju maksab (keslinna)?**
Take me to this address. **Viige mind sel aadressil.**
Where is the nearest bus stop? **Kus on lähim bussipeatus?**
When's the next bus to ...? **Millal läheb järmine buss ...?**
I want a ticket to ... **Palun üks pilet....sse.**
single/return **üks suund/edasitagasi**
How much is a ticket to (Tartu)? **Palju maksab pilet (Tartusse)?**
Will you tell me when to get off? **Kas te ütlete millal, ma pean maha minema?**

V

VISA AND ENTRY REQUIREMENTS

Passports/visas. Estonia is a member of the Schengen common visa area, so travellers coming from other Schengen countries will almost never have to undergo immigration or customs checks when crossing the border. That said, the law still requires that everyone brings valid travel documents and is able to produce them if asked. For visiting EU and EEA citizens, the document can be just a national ID card, but for all others, a valid passport is needed. When entering from outside Schengen, the above documents will be checked.

Citizens of the European Union, such as those from the UK, can enter Estonia freely. Citizens of the US, Canada, Australia and New Zealand can enter the Schengen zone and stay for up to 90 days in a six-month period without a visa. South Africans require Schengen visas. Contact the nearest Schengen country consulate to enquire about application procedures.

Regulations can change, so always check before you travel.

Customs. When arriving from outside the EU, you can import the usual 200 cigarettes, and 1 litre of hard alcohol or 2 litres of light alcohol (under 22 percent) without paying duties.

Exporting antiques. Antiques bought in Estonia cannot be exported without a permit. This applies to anything made in Estonia before 1945 and anything made elsewhere before 1850. Antique dealers should be able to assist you with the paperwork. Contact the National Heritage Board (tel: 6403 050; www.muinsuskaitseamet.ee) for information.

W

WEBSITES AND INTERNET

A few websites that will come in handy:

www.visittallinn.ee/eng The city's official tourism website, an excellent resource for travel planning.

www.visitestonia.com/en Estonia's official tourism website.

www.inyourpocket.com The extensive site of *Tallinn In Your Pocket*.

http://news.err.ee ERR News, by far the best source of daily local news in English.

www.vm.ee The Foreign Ministry's site, with interesting, general information on Estonia.

www.culture.ee A database of festivals and other events around the country.

www.ilm.ee Current weather conditions, as well as webcam views.

www.estonica.org The Encyclopedia Estonica, a slick, in-depth introduction to Estonian history, culture and society.

Free Wi-fi is found throughout the city. Nearly all cafes and restau-

rants offer free Wi-fi and there are also free public access points (you can see the map at: https://wifispc.com/estonia/harjumaa/tallinn.html)

Y

YOUTH HOSTELS

The **Estonian Youth Hostel Association** (Narva mnt. 16-25; tel: 6461 455; www.hostels.ee) provides most of its booking services through its website. Not all of the prominent hostels are listed, however.

Old Town hostels cater mainly to backpackers looking for a party atmosphere. Chief among these is **Tallinn Backpackers** (Olevimägi 11-1; tel: 6440 298; http://toth.ee/tallinn-backpackers). Australian-owned **Red Emperor Hostel** (Aia 10; tel: 6150 035; www.redemperorhostel.com) is another Old Town option. Not far away, **Euphoria** (Roosikrantsi 4; tel: 5837 3602; euphoria.traveller.ee) is a good alternative.

Farther out, the **GIDIC Hostel** (Tartu mnt. 31; tel: 6466 016; www.gidic.ee) offers decent beds in the downtown area. **Academic Hostel** (Akadeemia tee 11; tel: 6202 275; www.academichostel.com) is a large, modern hostel 5km (3 miles) from the city centre.

RECOMMENDED HOTELS

In the last decade, Tallinn's already world-class business and tourist hotels have been joined in the central-city skyline by a number of their high-rise brethren, apparently created with a 'bigger is better' philosophy in mind. Meanwhile, several Old Town buildings have been refashioned into intimate, luxury hotels and several speciality spa hotels have also cropped up.

The recent building trend focused on the middle to high end of the market, but with a bit of shopping around it is also possible to find a decently priced room in or close to Old Town. Additional budget options are available for anyone willing to brave a 10- or 15-minute taxi ride from the centre. There are also a number of tiny, out-of-the-way guesthouses; most are built onto private, suburban homes. Find them listed on the city's official tourism website, www.tourism.tallinn.ee.

The building boom has meant that accommodation shortages are a thing of the past, but prior booking is highly recommended for anyone planning to visit from May to August or at Christmas.

The symbols below have been used to indicate high-season rates, based on double occupancy with breakfast, VAT included. Hotels listed here have private showers/baths and accept major credit cards, unless otherwise indicated.

€€€€	Over €150
€€€	€100–€150
€€	€50–€100
€	Below €50

OLD TOWN

Baltic Hotel Imperial €€€€ *Nunne 14; tel: 6274 800;* www.imperial.ee. Part of the city's medieval wall runs right through this 19th-century building, but the Imperial creates most of its historic ambience with exposed brick and antique photos in its common areas. The hotel's pride and joy is definitely its magnificent, old-fashioned pub, but the sauna hall is also fairly impressive. Rooms are brightly decorated and have all the standard features. Laundry service is available. 32 rooms.

Baltic Hotel Vana Wiru €€€€ *Viru 11; tel: 6691 500;* www.vanawiru.ee. This modern hotel on the Old Town's main shopping street has an enviable location. It also offers an impressive lobby, two saunas, meeting rooms and a comfortable pub. Rooms are tasteful, but otherwise fairly standard, with all the features one would expect from a four-star establishment. Find the entrance around the back, accessible via Müürivahe Street. 82 rooms.

Barons €€€ *Suur-Karja 7/Väike-Karja 2; tel: 6999 700;* www.barons.ee. Steeped in elegance, this small, luxury hotel is in a 1912 former bank building (and it has the original vaults to prove it). Other interior details, including the charming wood-panelled lift, lobby bar, antique furniture and high ceilings, do a wonderful job of recreating the subdued primness of the early 20th century. 33 rooms.

Merchant's House Hotel €€€ *Dunkri 4/6; tel: 6977 500;* www.merchantshousehotel.com. Among the best of the boutique hotels, this elegant edifice just off Town Hall Square features top-notch rooms, some of which are tastefully decorated in a quasi-Asian style. These surround an inner courtyard café that provides a secluded spot for summer relaxation. In summer there is a lovely courtyard where you can relax with a glass of wine or a refreshing cocktail. 37 rooms.

Meriton Old Town Garden €€ *Pikk 29/Lai 24; tel: 6648 800;* www.meritonhotels.com. Meriton's newest Tallinn venture is a good choice for travellers who want to experience the comfort and charm of an Old Town boutique hotel at a more reasonable cost. One of its two entrances faces the busy, restaurant- and bar-filled Pikk Street, and the other is on the quieter Lai street, where the hotel operates its own courtyard café. Tempting cakes are sold in the hotel's own bakery. 50 rooms.

My City Hotel €€€ *Vana-Posti 11/13; tel: 6220 900;* www.mycityhotel.ee. One look at the marble columns and grand chandeliers in the lobby is enough to show that the owners took extra pains to make this a chic establishment. All 68 rooms are decorated in a smart, vaguely old-fashioned way, but each comes with its own computer as well as mini-bar, safe and hairdryer. Suites come complete with kitchenettes.

OldHouse Guesthouse/OldHouse Hostel € *Uus 22/Uus 26; tel: 6411 281;* www.oldhouse.ee. Do not read too much into the 'guesthouse' and 'hostel' labels here – amenities and prices in these twin establishments are nearly identical. Each offers simple, modern single and double rooms, as well as larger 'dorm-style' rooms, all with shared bathrooms. The only discernible difference between the two is that the 'hostel' is a touch nicer and has two more of the large rooms. The price includes breakfast and use of the guest kitchen. 6 rooms (guesthouse), 12 rooms (hostel). This family-owned company also runs 29 fully equipped apartments in the Old Town.

Olevi Residents €€€ *Olevimägi 4; tel: 6277 650;* www.olevi.ee. The charmingly narrow, 14th-century building alone is enough to create a timeless atmosphere, but the little Olevi hotel is also overflowing with antique-style furnishings and decor. The establishment also features a small restaurant serving European dishes with a modern twist. 37 rooms.

Schlössle €€€€ *Pühavaimu 13/15; tel: 6997 700;* www.schlossle-hotels. com. An elder figure in Tallinn's pantheon of small, luxury hotels, the Schlössle earns its five-star rating with a combination of impressive ambience and impeccable service. Ancient stone and heavy wooden beams give the lobby its medieval look, while rooms are furnished in a lavish, antique style – right down to the polished brass taps. The long list of amenities includes bathrobes, complimentary daily newspapers and a babysitting service. 23 rooms.

St Petersbourg €€€ *Rataskaevu 7; tel: 6286 500;* www.hotelstpeters bourg.com. Run by the same group that manages the respected Schlössle, this hotel spoils its guests with similar, old-fashioned comforts, as well as an upmarket Russian restaurant and a simpler Estonian restaurant. Operating since the late 19th century, the St Petersbourg is Tallinn's oldest hotel, and decorators have done a good job of recreating the aristocratic sophistication of that era. Rooms are art deco in style. Be warned that standard rooms are tiny. 27 rooms.

Telegraaf €€€€ *Vene 9; tel: 6000 600;* www.telegraafhotel.com. A relatively recent addition to Tallinn's luxury hotel scene, this five-star establishment makes its home in a building that housed a bank and a telegraph exchange in the late-19th and early 20th centuries. The hotel has incorporated that feeling of tsarist-era elegance into its chic decor, as well as in its acclaimed Tchaikovsky restaurant (see page 109). It also offers more extras than is typical of Old Town hotels, including spa facilities. 83 rooms.

The Three Sisters €€€€ *Pikk 71/Tolli 2; tel: 6306 300;* http://www.3s.ee. Built inside Tallinn's famous Three Sisters, a trio of 14th–15th-century houses, this five-star hotel offers unmatched lavishness, from the real candles used in the lobby chandelier to the amazing in-room decor. In addition to the standard amenities, each of the 23 rooms comes with luxury furniture, CD and DVD player, bathrobe and an umbrella. Some rooms have king-sized poster beds and one suite even has its own piano.

CITY CENTRE

Braavo Spa Hotel €€ *Aia 20; tel: 6999 777;* www.braavohotel.com. Young people and families in particular will appreciate the spacious, cheerful rooms offered in this small hotel at the edge of Old Town. Its reception is shared with a busy sports club, offering opportunities for a swim or a workout. And while the parking-lot views are nothing to write home about, the location, so close to Old Town, is hard to beat. The water park and spa make it an ideal place for families. 38 rooms.

Go Hotel Schnelli €€ *Toompuiestee 37; tel: 6310 100;* www.gohotels.ee. This modern hotel attached to the train station is a popular choice for its balance of price and location – just outside the walls of Old Town. Some rooms face the railway tracks while others have stunning views of Toompea Hill – be sure to specify your preference when booking. A walkway connects it to the station itself, where the hotel operates a day spa and chic café. 124 rooms.

Kreutzwald Hotel Tallinn €€€ *Endla 23, tel: 6664 800,* www.kreutzwald hotel.com. Run by the same group that created the respected Von Stackelberg, the larger Kreutzwald makes its home in a renovated, 1950s-era building about five minutes farther by foot from the Old Town. It offers similar ultra-smart rooms and spa services as well as a library lounge and a Brazilian restaurant. 65 rooms.

Meriton Grand Conference & Spa Hotel €€€ *Paldiski mnt. 4; tel: 6677 111;* www.meritonhotels.com. Sitting on the opposite edge of the Old Town from Tallinn's main commercial centre, the Grand is not in the middle of the action. Still, it is within easy walking distance of the town's main sights and has some excellent views of nearby Toompea Castle. Guests staying in either of its two large buildings can take advantage of the spa centre, top-notch restaurants, and a host of services, ranging from conference facilities to dental treatment. 465 rooms.

Nordic Hotel Forum €€€ *Viru väljak 3; tel: 6222 900;* www.nordichotels. eu. Though it makes much of its trade from business travellers, the Nordic Forum is an excellent choice for sightseers as well thanks to its prime, central location, high-quality rooms and range of services. Some rooms even come equipped with Skype phones to let guests stay in touch. It also boasts a top-notch restaurant and a relaxation centre. 267 rooms.

Radisson BLU Hotel Olümpia €€€ *Liivalaia 33; tel: 6315 333;* www.radisson blu.com/olumpiahotel-tallinn. This four-star monolith is contemporary looking inside and out despite the fact it was built for the 1980 Olympic Games. With 390 rooms and an attached conference centre, it is one of the biggest hotels in Tallinn, drawing large groups. The hotel also has business facilities, a comfortable restaurant, lunch café and a pub. In the health club on the 26th floor guests can use a sauna and swimming pool while taking in spectacular views of the city. The hotel is 10–15 minutes' walk from the Old Town. 390 rooms.

Radisson BLU Hotel Tallinn €€€ *Rävala pst. 3; tel: 6823 000;* www.radisson blu.com/hotel-tallinn. Tallinn's most gleaming Radisson, a five-minute walk from the Old Town, delivers everything one would expect from a world-class chain hotel. The towering building is the tallest in the city, so ask for a room on the town side for the most interesting views. Rooms are decorated in Oriental, Italian, Maritime or Scandinavian themes. A large number of conference rooms are available, as are business services, a health club and a cigar shop. The hotel also operates two restaurants and, in summer, a rooftop café. 280 rooms.

Hotel Palace €€ *Vabaduse väljak 3; tel: 6407 200;* www.tallinnhotels.ee/ hotel-palace-tallinn. A strong dose of 1930s-style class has worked its way into every corner of this historic building, which stands just outside the Old Town and overlooks Freedom Square. It is starting to seem a bit scruffy compared to recent, super-modern four-star arrivals, but few can beat its authentic feel, location or welcoming lobby bar. It also has a sauna, conference facilities and, in some rooms, air conditioning. 79 rooms.

Sokos Viru Hotel €€–€€€ *Viru väljak 4; tel: 6809 300;* www.sokoshotels. com. Tallinn's most famous Soviet-era high-rise hotel has evolved into a quality, international establishment that is especially popular with Finnish tour groups. Apart from its enviable location beside the Old Town, the gigantic, Finnish-run hotel offers colourfully decorated rooms, a conference centre, saunas, gym, a beauty salon, countless bars, an upmarket restaurant, a casual Tex-Mex restaurant, and a nightclub. The Viru is also conveniently attached to downtown's largest shopping and dining complex, the Viru Centre. 516 rooms.

Swissôtel Tallinn €€€–€€€€ *Tornimäe 3; tel: 6240 000;* www.swissotel. com/tallinn. Built in a skyscraper that dominates the centre of the city's financial district (a mere 10-minute walk from Old Town), the Estonian branch of this respected international chain beats its rivals for amenities, services and all-around lavishness. A restaurant with a view, a spa centre and little touches like in-room espresso machines are what sets it apart. Ask for a room overlooking Old Town. 238 rooms.

Von Stackelberg Hotel Tallinn €€€€ *Toompuiestee 23; tel: 6600 700;* www.uhotelsgroup.com. This modern hotel makes its home in a brick building on the quiet edge of the Old Town, not far from Toompea Castle. The concept here is to offer guests something unique, specifically rooms with tasteful, chic designs and their own computers. For an extra fee, guests can opt for one of the Zen rooms, which have such extras as aromatherapy amenities and adjustable lighting. The hotel also has two good cafés. 52 rooms.

PORT AREA

City Hotel Portus €–€€ *Uus-Sadama 23; tel: 6806 600;* www.tallinn hotels.ee. There is a decidedly hip, dynamic edge to the interior design and the service at Portus, but the real strengths of this 107-room hotel are the location, across from the passenger port's D-Terminal, and the huge number of extras for the price. These include a sauna, free internet terminals in the lobby and a children's playroom. There is also the rock-and-roll-themed Café Retro, where you can get pizzas, burgers and the like. Rooms are stylish, with cork floors, satellite TV and wireless internet connection.

Hestia Hotel Ilmarine €€€ *Põhja pst. 21b; tel: 6818 878;* http://pk-ilmarine-hotel.hotelintallinn.com. A top-notch hotel cleverly built into a late 19th-century industrial complex. Forty-six of its 105 rooms are split-level. These surround an indoor atrium and have park or sea views and their own kitchenettes. All rooms are equipped with either wireless or fixed-line internet connections, and computers can be requested. The hotel also offers meeting rooms, sauna, a restaurant, lounge and café.

Tallink Express € *Sadama 9; tel: 6678 700;* www.tallinkhotels.com. Located just a few metres from Tallinn's main passenger port, this modern hotel caters mainly to ferry passengers looking for economy and convenience. It does not offer much in the way of extra services, but rooms are fully furnished and immaculately clean, service is very professional, and the café's well-known soup buffet is a true bargain. 166 rooms.

Tallink Spa & Conference Hotel €€ *Sadama 11a; tel: 6301 000;* www. hotels.tallink.com. Designed primarily to let ferry travellers pamper themselves without having to venture too far from the port, this hotel is also a good option for sightseers thanks to its proximity to Fat Margaret's Tower and Old Town. Visitors can make a splash in the aqua centre and try out the in-pool bar. Those with relaxation in mind should enquire about the available Spa packages. 275 rooms.

FURTHER AFIELD

Birgitta Guesthouse €–€€ *Merevälja tee 18; tel: 6055 000; www.birgitta guesthouse.ee.* The nuns of the Catholic Bridgettine Order operate this 20-room guesthouse in the Pirita beach district, 10–15 minutes' drive from the centre. The modern facility overlooks the fascinating ruins of the 15th-century St Bridget's Convent, often the site of classical concerts in summer. Each room is modern, comfortable and has its own shower and phone. The TV and kitchen are shared. Cash only.

Dzingel € *Männiku tee 89; tel: 6105 201; www.dzingel.ee.* This sprawling hotel in the pine-filled Nõmme district is popular with budget tourists who do not mind travelling the 6km (4 miles) to and from the city centre. While not as flashy as its more central rivals, the Dzingel offers a modern grill restaurant, saunas, conference rooms, an 'internet corner' and spa treatments. Its 285 rooms are standard and more than adequate. There is a convenient bus connection.

Ecoland €€ *Randvere tee 115; tel: 6051 999; www.ecoland.ee.* Old-fashioned designs, parrots, goldfish and an endless jumble of antiques create an almost storybook feel in this boutique hotel. Rooms have phone, cable TV and showers with heated floors. Morning sauna and use of the swimming pool are included in the price. Restaurant, laundry and dry-cleaning services are also available. The hotel is 15–20 minutes by car from the centre. 81 rooms.

Tähetorni €€ *Tähetorni 16; tel: 6779 100; www.thotell.ee.* From the outside Tähetorni has the appearance of a tiny castle, while the interior of this fairly new brick structure is a labyrinth of odd hallways and spiral staircases. Guests have a bar, sauna, conference rooms and a restaurant with an outside terrace at their disposal. Rooms are large and fully equipped. The hotel is 9km (6 miles) from the centre. 35 rooms.

DICTIONARY

ENGLISH–ESTONIAN

adj adjective   **adv** adverb   **BE** British English   **n** noun   **prep** preposition   **v** verb

A

accept v aktsep-
teerima
access n ligipääs
accident n õnnetus
accommodation
majutus
account n (bank)
konto (pangakonto)
acupuncture aku-
punktuur
adapter adapter
address n aadress
admission (price)
vastuvõtt (hind)
after pärast; **~noon**
pärastlõuna; **~shave**
lualettvoci
age n vanus
agency agentuur
AIDS AIDS
air n õhk;
~ conditioning
õhukonditsioneer;
~-dry õhkkuivatus;
~ pump õhupump;
~line lonnuliin·
~mail lennupost;
~plane lennuk;
~port lennujaam
aisle vahekäik;
~ seat vahek-
äigupoolne koht

allergic allergiline;
~ reaction allergiline
reaktsioon
allow lubama
alone üksinda
alter v muutma
alternate route alternatiivne marsruut
aluminum foil alumi-
iniumfoolium
amazing hämmastav
ambulance kiirabi
American adj
ameerika
amusement park
lõbustuspark
anemic aneemiline
anesthesia anesteesia
animal loom
ankle pahkluu
antibiotic n anti-
biootikum
antiques store
antiikesemete pood
antiseptic cream
antiseptiline kreem
apartment korter
appendix (body part)
pimesool
appetizer eelroog
appointment
kohtumine
arcade arkaad

area code suunakood
arm n (body part)
käsi
aromatherapy
aroomiteraapia
around (the corner)
ümber (nurga);
~ (price) soovitatav
hind
arrival saabumine
arrive saabuma
artery arter
arthritis liigese-
põletik
art kunst
Asian adj aasialik
aspirin aspiriin
asthmatic astmaatik
ATM sularahaau-
tomaat; **~ card**
ATM-kaart
attack v ründama
attraction (place)
atraktsioon
attractive veetlev
Australia Austraalia
Australian adj
austraalia
automatic
automaatne; **~ car**
automaatkäigu-
kastiga auto
available saadaval

B

baby beebi; **~ bottle**
beebipudel; **~ wipe**
beebisalvrätik· **~sit-**
ter lapsehoidja
back (body part) selg;
~ache seljavalu;
~pack seljakott
bag kott
baggage [BE]
pagas; **~ claim**
pagasi kättesaamine;
~ ticket pagasi pilet
hake v küpsetama
bakery pagariäri
ballet ballett
bandage side
bank n pank
bar (place) baar
barbecue (device)
n grill
barber habemeajaja
baseball pesapall
basket (grocery store)
korv
basketball korvpall
bathroom vannituba
battery patarei
ballleground
lahinguväli
be v olema
beach rand
beautiful ilus

bed *n* voodi; **~ and breakfast** öömaja hommikusöögiga

before enne

begin algama

beginner algaja

behind (direction) taga

beige *adj* beež

belt vöö

best *adj* parim; **~ before** parim enne

better parem

bicycle jalgratas

big suur; **~ger** suurem

bike route jalgrattatee

bikini bikiinid

bill *n* **(money)** rahatäht; **~ n (of sale)** ostu-müügileping

bird lind

birthday sünnipäev

black *adj* must

bladder põis

bland maitsetu

blanket tekk

bleed veritsema

blender kannmikser

blood veri; **~ pressure** vererõhk

blouse pluus

blue *adj* sinine

board *v* pardale astuma; **~ing pass** pardapääse

boat *n* paat

boil *v* keetma

bone *n* luu

book *n* raamat; **~store** raamatupood

boot *n* saabas

boring igav

botanical garden botaanikaaed

bother *v* tüütama

bottle *n* pudel; **~ opener** pudeliavaja

bowl *n* kauss

boxing match poksimatš

boy poiss; **~friend** poiss-sõber

bra rinnahoidja

bracelet käevõru

brake (car) pidur

breaded paneeritud

break *v* **(bone)** murdma

breakdown (car) rike

breakfast *n* hommikusöök

break-in (burglary) *n* sissemurdmine

breast rind; **~feed** *v* rinnaga toitma

breathe hingama

bridge sild

briefs (clothing) aluspüksid

bring tooma

British *adj* briti

broken katkine; **~ (bone)** luumurd

brooch pross

broom luud

brother vend

brown *adj* pruun

bug (insect) *n* putukas

building hoone

burn *v* põletama

bus *n* buss; **~ station** bussijaam; **~ stop** bussipeatus; **~ ticket** bussipilet; **~ tour** bussireis

business *adj* äri; **~ card** ärikaart; **~ center** ärikeskus; **~ class** äriklass; **~ hours** lahtiolekuaeg

butcher lihunik

buttocks istmik

buy *v* ostma

bye nägemist

C

cabaret kabaree

cable car tõstuk

cafe (place) kohvik

call *v* **(phone)** helistama; **~** *n* kõne; **~ collect** kõne vastuvõtja kulul

calorie kalor

camera kaamera; **~ case** kaamerakott

digital ~ digitaalne kaamera

camp *v* telkima; **~ing stove** telkimispliit; **~site** telkimisplats

can opener konservikarbiavaja

Canada Kanada

Canadian *adj* kanada

cancel tühistama

candy komm

canned good konservtoit

canyon kanjon

car auto; **~ hire [BE]**

autorent; **~ park [BE]** parkla; **~ rental** auto rentimine; **~ seat** autoiste

carafe karahvin

card *n* kaart

ATM ~ ATM-kaart

credit ~ krediitkaart

debit ~ deebetkaart

phone ~ telefonikaart

carry-on *n* **(piece of hand luggage)** käsipagas

cart (grocery store) käru; **~ (luggage)** pagasikäru

carton (of cigarettes) sigaretipakk; **~ (of groceries)** pakend

cash *n* sularaha; **~** *v* rahaks tegema

cashier kassapidaja

casino kasiino

castle loss

cathedral katedraal

cave *n* koobas

CD CD

cell phone mobiiltelefon

Celsius Celsius

centimeter sentimeeter

certificate tunnistus

chair *n* tool; **~ lift** tõstuk

change *v* **(baby)** mähkmeid vahetama; **~ (buses)** busse vahetama; **~ (money)** raha vahetama; **~** *n* **(money)** peenraha

charge v (credit card) tasu võtma; ~ (cost) hind

cheap odav; **~er** odavam

check v (luggage) kontrollima; ~ (on something) kontrollima; n (payment) tšekk; **~-in** sisseregistreerimine; **~ing account** jooksevkonto; **~-out** väljaregistreerimine

Cheers! Terviseks!

chemical toilet keemiline tualett

chemist [BE] keemik

chest (body part) rind; **~ pain** rinnavalu

chewing gum närimiskumm

child laps; **~'s seat** lapseiste

children's menu lastemenüü

children's portion lapse ports

Chinese adj hiina

chopsticks söögipulgad

church kirik

cigar sigar

class n klass; **~ business ~** äriklass; **~ economy** turistiklass; **~ first** esimene klass

classical music klassikaline muusika

clean v koristama;

~ adj (clothes) puhas; **~ing product** puhastusvahend

clear v (on an ATM) võlga tasuma

cliff kalju

cling film [BE] kile

close v (a shop) sulgema

closed kinnine

clothing riietus; **~ store** riietepood

club n klubi

coat mantel

coin münt

colander sõel

cold n (sickness) haigus; **~** adj (temperature) külm

colleague kolleeg

cologne lõhnavesi

color n värv

comb n kamm

come v tulema

complaint kaebus

computer arvuti

concert kontsert; **~ hall** kontserdihall

condition (medical) konditsioon, seisund

conditioner (hair) palsam

condom kondoom

conference konverents

confirm kinnitama

congestion (medical) kongestioon

connect (internet) ühendama

connection (travel/internet) ühendus;

~ flight ühenduslend

constipated kõhukinnisuse all kannatav

consulate konsulaat

consultant konsultant

contact v ühendust võtma

contact lens kontaktlääts; **~ solution** läätsevedelik

contagious nakkav

convention hall kokkutulekusaal

conveyor belt konveierilint

cook v küpsetama

cool adj (temperature) jahe

copper n vask

corkscrew n korgitser

cost v maksma

cotton puuvill

cough v köhima; **~** n köha

country code riigi kood

cover charge restorani lisatasu

cream (ointment) kreem

credit card krediitkaart

crew neck sirge kaelus

crib võrevoodi

crystal n (glass) kristall

cup n tass

currency valuuta; **~ exchange** valuutavahetus; **~ exchange office** valuutavahe-

tuspunkt

current account [BE] jooksevkonto

customs toll

cut v lõikama; **~** n (injury) haav

cute armas

cycling rattasõit

D

damage v kahjustama

dance v tantsima; **~ club** tantsuklubi; **~ing** tantsimine

dangerous ohtlik

dark adj pime

date n (calendar) kuupäev

day päev

deaf adj kurt

debit card deebetkaart

deck chair lamamistool

declare v (customs) deklareerima

decline v (credit card) keelduma

deep adj sügav

degree (temperature) kraad

delay v viivitama

delete v (computer) kustutama

delicatessen delikatessid

delicious maitsev

denim teksasriie

dentist hambaarst

denture kunsthammas

deodorant deodorant

department store kaubamaja

departure-(plane)
väljasõit

deposit *v* **(money)**
sissemaksu tegema;
~ *n* **(bank)** deposiit

desert *n* kõrb

detergent puhastus-
vahend

develop *v* **(film)**
ilmutama

diabetic *adj* diabeetiline; ~ *n* diabeetik

dial *v* numbrit valima

diamond teemant

diaper mähe

diarrhea kõhulahtisus

diesel diisel

difficult keeruline

digital digitaalne;
~ **camera** digitaalne
kaamera; ~ **photo**
digitaalne foto;
~ **print** digitaaltrükk

dining room
söögituba

dinner õhtusöök

direction suund

dirty räpane

disabled *adj* **(person)**
puudega; ~ **ac-
cessible [BE]**
puuetega inimestele
juurdepääs

**disconnect (comput-
er)** välja lülitama,
lahti ühendama

discount *n* al-
lahindlus

dishes (kitchen) nõud

dishwasher nõudepe-
sumasin

dishwashing liquid

nõudepesuvedelik

display *n* **(device)**
kuvar; ~ **case** vitriin

disposable *n*
äravisatav; ~ **razor**
ühekordselt kasu-
tatav raseerija

dive *v* sukelduma

diving equipment
sukeldumisvarustus

divorce *v* lahutama

dizzy *adj* peapööritav

doctor *n* arst

doll *n* nukk

dollar (U.S.) dollar

domestic kodumaine;
~ **flight** siseliinilend

door uks

dormitory ühiselamu

double bed kaheini-
mesevoodi

downtown *n* kesklinn

dozen tosin

drag lift suusatõstuk

dress (clothing) kleit;
~ **code** riietumisstiil

drink *v* jooma;
~ *n* jook; ~ **menu**
joogimenüü; ~**ing
water** joogivesi

drive *v* sõitma

**driver's license
number** juhiloa
number

drop *n* **(medicine)**
tilguti

drowsiness unisus

dry clean keemiline
puhastus; ~**er's**
keemiline puhastus

dubbed dubleeritud

during ajal

duty (tax) tollimaks;
~**-free** maksuvaba

DVD DVD

E

ear kõrv; ~**ache**
kõrvavalu

earlier enne

early varajane

earring kõrvarõngas

east *n* ida

easy lihtne

eat *v* sööma

economy class
turistiklass

elbow *n* küünarnukk

electric outlet
pistikupesa

elevator lift

e-mail *v* e-kirja
saatma; ~ *n* e-kiri;
~ **address** e-posti
aadress

emergency erakor-
raline olukord; ~ **exit**
varuväljapääs

empty *v* tühjendama

end *v* lõpetama;
~ *n* lõpp

engaged (person)
kihlatud

English *adj* inglise; ~ *n*
(language) inglise
keel

engrave graveerima

enjoy nautima

enter *v* **(place)**
sisenema

entertainment
meelelahutus

entrance sissepääs

envelope ümbrik

epileptic *adj* epileptiline; ~ *n* epileptik

equipment varustus

escalator eskalaator

e-ticket e-pilet

EU resident ELi
resident

euro euro

evening *n* õhtu

excess baggage
lisapagas

exchange *v* vahetus;
~ *n* **(place)** valuuta-
vahetuspunkt; ~ **rate**
vahetuskurss

excursion ekskursioon

excuse *v* vabandama

exhausted kurnatud

exit *v* väljuma; ~ *n*
väljapääs

expensive kallis

experienced kogenud

expert ekspert

exposure (film)
säritus

express *adj* selgesõnaline; ~ **bus** ek-
spressbuss; ~ **train**
ekspressrong

extension (phone)
parallteletelefon

extra *adj* lisa; ~ **large**
ekstra suur

extract *v* **(tooth)** välja
tõmbama

eye silm

eyebrow wax
kulmuvaha

F

face *n* nägu

facial *n* näohooldus

family n perekond

fan n (appliance) ventilaator

far (distance) kaugel

farm farm

far-sighted kauge-lenägelik

fast adj kiire

fat free rasvavaba

father isa

fax v faksi saatma; ~ n faks; **~ number** faksinumber

fee n tasu

feed v toitma

ferry n praam

fever n palavik

field (sports) väljak

fill v (car) tankima

fill out v (form) täitma

filling (tooth) plomm

film n (camera) film

fine n (fee for breaking law) trahv

finger n sõrm; **~nail** sõrmeküüs

fire n tuli; **~ department** tuletõrje; **~ door** tulekindel uks

first adj esimene; **~ class** esimene klass

fit n (clothing) ümber keha riided

fitting room proovikabiin

fix v (repair) parandama

fixed-price menu fikseeritud hindadega menüü

flash photography välgu kasutamine pildistamiseks

flashlight taskulamp

flight n lend

flip-flops plätud

floor n (level) korrus

florist lillekaupmees

flower n lill

folk music rahvamuusika

food toit; **~ processor** köögikombain

foot n jalg

football game [BE] jalgpallimäng

for eest

forecast n ennustus

forest n mets

fork n kahvel

form n (document) vorm

formula (baby) beebitoit

fort kindlustus

fountain n purskkaev

free adj vaba

freelance work vabakutseline töötaja

freezer külmik

fresh värske

friend sõber

frozen food külmutatud toit

frying pan praepann

full-time adj põhikohaga

G

game n mäng

garage n (parking) garaaž; ~ n (for re-

pairs) autotöökoda

garbage bag prügikott

gas (car) bensiin; **~ station** bensiinijaam

gate (airport) värav

gay adj (homosexual) ilmc ravim gei; **~ bar** geibaar; **~ club** geiklubi

gel n (hair) geel

generic drug geneeriline ravim

German adj saksa; ~ n (language) saksa keel

Germany Saksamaa

get off (a train/bus/subway) maha minema

gift n kink; **~ shop** kingipood

girl tüdruk; **~friend** tüdruksõber

give v andma

glass (drinking) klaas; **~ (material)** klaas

glasses prillid

go v (somewhere) minema

gold n kuld

golf n golf; **~ course** golfirada; **~ tournament** golfiturniir

good adj hea; **~ afternoon** tere päevast; **~ day** head päeva; **~ evening** tere õhtust; **~ morning** tere hommikust; **~bye** nägemist

gram gramm

grandchild lapselaps

grandparents vanavanemad

gray adj hall

green adj roheline

grocery store toidupood

ground floor esimene korrus

groundcloth telgi põhi

group n grupp

guide n (book) juhend; ~ n (person) giid; **~ dog** juhtkoer

gym n (place) jõusaal

gynecologist günekoloog

H

hair juuksed; **~brush** juuksehari; **~cut** juukselõikus; **~ dryer** föön; **~ salon** juuksurisalong; **~spray** juukselakk; **~style** soeng; **~ stylist** stilist

halal halal, lubatud

half adj pooleldi; ~ n pool; **~ hour** pooltund; **~-kilo** pool kilo

hammer n haamer

hand n käsi; **~ luggage** käsipagas; **~ wash** käsitsipesu; **~bag [BE]** käekott

handicapped puudega; **~-accessible** puuetega inimeste juurdepääs

hangover pohmell
happy õnnelik
hat müts
have v omama; ~ **sex** seksima
hay fever heinapalavik
head (body part) n pea; ~**ache** peavalu; ~**phones** kõrvaklapid
health tervis; ~ **food store** tervisliku toidu pood
hearing impaired kuulmispuudega
heart süda; ~ **condition** haige süda
heat v soojendama; ~**er** kütteheha; ~**ing** [BE] soojendamine
hectare hektar
hello tere
helmet kiiver
help v aitama; ~ n abi
here siin
hi tere
high kõrge; ~**chair** lastetool; ~**lights (hair)** salgud; ~**way** maantee
hiking boots mat-kasaapad
hill n küngas
hire v [BE] (a car) rentima; ~ **car** [BE] rendiauto
hockey hoki
holiday [BE] puhkus
horsetrack hobuserada
hospital haigla
hostel kämping
hot (spicy) vürtsikas; ~ **(temperature)**

kuum; ~ **spring** kuumaveeallikas; ~ **water** soe vesi
hotel hotell
hour tund
house n maja; ~**hold goods** majapidam-istarbed; ~**keeping services** majapidam-isteenused
how kuidas, kui; ~ **much** kui palju
hug v kallistama
hungry näljane
hurt v haiget tegema
husband abikaasa

I

ibuprofen ibuprofeen
ice n jää; ~ **hockey** jäähoki
icy jäine
identification tunnus
ill haige
in sees
include v sisaldama
indoor pool (public) sisebassein
inexpensive odav
infected saastatud
information (phone) infotelefon; ~ **desk** infopunkt
insect putukas; ~ **bite** putukahammustus; ~ **repellent** putu-katõrjevahend
insert v (card) sisestama
insomnia unetus
instant message kiirsõnum

insulin insuliin
insurance kindlustus; ~ **card** kindlus-tuskaart; ~ **company** kindlustusselts
interesting huvitav
intermediate kes-kmine
international rahvus-vaheline; ~ **flight** rahvusvaheline lend; ~ **student card** rahvusvaheline õpilaskaart
internet Internet; ~ **cafe** interneti-punkt; ~ **service** interneti-teenus
interpreter tõlk
intersection ristmik
intestine seedekulgla
introduce v (person) tutvustama
invoice n [BE] arve
Ireland lirimaa
Irish adj iiri
iron v triikima; ~ n (clothes) triikraud
Italian adj itaalia

J

jacket n pintsak
Japanese adj jaapani
jar n (for jam etc.) purk
jaw n lõug
jazz n džäss; ~ **club** džässiklubi
jeans teksad
jet ski n jeti
jeweler juveliir
jewelry kalliskivid

join v (go with some-body) ühinema
joint n (body part) liiges

K

key n võti; ~ **card** võtmekaart; ~**ring** võtmehoidja
kiddie pool lastebas-sein
kidney (body part) neer
kilo kilo; ~**gram** kilogramm; ~**meter** kilomeeter
kiss v suudlema
kitchen köök; ~ **foil** [BE] köögifoolium
knee n põlv
knife nuga
kosher adj seaduslik, lubatud

L

lace n (fabric) pits
lactose intolerant laktoositalumatu
lake järv
large suur
last adj viimane
late (time) hiline
launderette [BE] iseteenindusp-esumaja
laundromat pesumaja
laundry (place) pesumaja; ~ **service** pesupesemisteenus
lawyer n advokaat
leather n nahk

leave v (hotel) lahkuma; ~ (plane) välja astuma
left adj, adv (direction) vasak
leg n jalg
lens lääts
less vähem
lesson n õppetund
take ~s võle/võtted
letter n kiri
library raamatukogu
life jacket päästevest
lifeguard vetelpäästja
lift n [BE] lift; ~ n (ride) tõstuk; ~ **pass** suusatõstuki pilet
light n (cigarette) tuli; ~ n (overhead) valgusti; ~**bulb** lamp
lighter n välgumihkel
like v meeldima
line n (train/bus) liin
linen lina
lip n huul
liquor store alkoholipood
liter liiter
little väike
live v elama; ~ **music** elav muusika
liver (body part) maks
loafers sandaalid
local n (person) kohalik
lock v lukustama; ~ n lukk
locker hoiukapp
log off v (computer) välja logima

log on v (computer) sisse logima
long adj pikk; ~**-sighted** [BE] kaugnägelik; ~**-sleeved** pikkade käistega
look v otsima; ~ **for something** otsima midagi
loose (fit) avar
lose v (something) kaotama
lost kadunud; ~**-and-found** leiubüroo
lotion ihupiim
louder kõvemini
love v (someone) armastama; ~ n armastus
low adj madal
luggage pagas; ~ **cart** pagasikäru; ~ **locker** pagasilaegas; ~ **ticket** pagasipilet
lunch n lõuna
lung kops
luxury car luksusauto

M

machine washable masinpestav
magazine ajakiri
magnificent suurepärane
mail v kirja saatma; ~ n kiri; ~**box** postkast
main attraction peamine atraktsioon
main course põhiroog
mall kaubanduskeskus

man (adult male) mees
manager juhataja
manicure n maniküür
manual car manuaalkäigukastiga auto
map n kaart; ~ n (town) linnakaart
market n turg
married abielus
marry abielluma
mass n (church service) missa
massage n massaaž
match n tikk
meal n eine
measure v (someone) mõõtma
measuring cup mõõdutass
measuring spoon mõõtelusikas
mechanic n mehaanik
medication (drugs) ravim
medicine meditsiin
medium (steak) keskmiselt läbipraetud
meet v kohtuma
meeting n (business) koosolek; ~ **room** koosolekuruum
membership card liikmekaart
memorial (place) mälestusmärk
memory card mälukaart
mend v (clothes) parandama
menstrual cramps

menstruatsioonikrambid
menu (restaurant) menüü
message sõnum
meter n (parking) arvesti; ~ n (measure) meeter
microwave n mikrolaineahi
midday [BE] lõuna
midnight kesköö
mileage läbisõit
mini-bar minibaar
minute minut
missing (not there) puuduv
mistake n viga
mobile home mobiilne kodu
mobile phone [BE] mobiiltelefon
mobility liikuvus
monastery klooster
money raha
month kuu
mop n mopp
moped mopeed
more rohkem
morning n hommik
mosque mošee
mother n ema
motion sickness merehaigus
motor n mootor; ~ **boat** mootorpaat; ~**cycle** mootorratas; ~**way** [BE] maantee
mountain mägi; ~ **bike** mägiratas
mousse (hair) vaht
mouth n suu

movie film; **~ theater** kino
mug v röövima
multiple-trip ticket mitme reisi pilet
muscle n lihas
museum muuseum
music muusika; **~ store** muusikapood

N

nail file küüneviil
nail salon küüne-salong
name n nimi
napkin salvrätt
nappy [BE] mähe
nationality rahvus
nature preserve looduskaitseala
nausea iiveldus
nauseous iiveldav
near lähedal; **~-sighted** lühinägelik
nearby lähedal
neck n kael
necklace kaelakee
need v vajama
newspaper ajaleht
newsstand ajale-hekiosk
next adj järgmine
nice kena
night öö; **~club** ööklubi
no ei; **~ (not any)** mitte ühtegi
non-alcoholic mit-tealkohoolne
non-smoking adj mittesuitsetav
noon n lõuna

north n põhi
nose nina
note n [BE] (money) rahatäht
nothing mitte miski
notify v teavitama
novice uustulnuk
now nüüd
number n number
nurse n õde

O

office kontor; **~ hours** lahtiolekuaeg
off-licence [BE] veinipood
oil n õli
OK OK
old adj vana
on the corner nurga peal
once (one time) kord
one (counting) üks; **~-day (ticket)** ühe päeva pilet; **~-way ticket (airline)** ühe otsa pilet (lennuk); **~-(bus/train/sub-way)** ühe otsa pilet (buss, rong, metroo); **~-way street** ühesuunaline tänav
only ainult
open v avama; **~ adj** avatud
opera ooper; **~ house** ooperiteater
opposite n vastand
optician optik
orange adj (color) oranž
orchestra orkester

order v (restaurant) tellimus
outdoor pool välibas-sein
outside prep väljas
over prep (direction) üle; **~done (meat)** ülepraetud; **~heat** v (car) ülekuumene-nud; **~look** n (scenic place) vaade; **~night** üleöö; **~-the-counter (medica-tion)** retseptita
oxygen treatment hapnikuravi

P

p.m. p.m.
pacifier lutt
pack v pakkima
package n pakend
pad n [BE] padi
paddling pool [BE] lastebassein
pain valu
pajamas pidžaama
palace palee
pants püksid
pantyhose sukkpüksid
paper n (material) paber; **~ towel** paberkäterätt
paracetamol [BE] paratsetamool
park v parkima; **~ n** park; **~ing garage** garaaž; **~ing lot** parkla; **~ing meter** parkimisau-tomaat
parliament building

parlamendihoone
part (for car) osa; **~-time** adj poole kohaga
pass through v (travel) läbi reisima
passenger reisija
passport pass; **~ con-trol** passikontroll
password salasõna
pastry shop kondiitri-toodete pood
patch v (clothing) paikama
path rada
pay v maksma; **~phone** telefoniau-tomaat
peak n (of a mountain) tipp
pearl n pärl
pedestrian n jalakäija
pediatrician lastearst
pedicure n pediküür
pen n sulepea
penicillin penitsilliin
penis peenis
per kohta; **~ day** päevas; **~ hour** tunnis; **~ night** öös; **~ week** nädalas
perfume n parfüüm
period (menstrual) menstruatsioon; **~ (of time)** periood
permit v lubama
petrol [BE] bensiin; **~ station [BE]** ben-siinijaam
pewter tinasulam
pharmacy apteek, farmaatsia

phone v helistama; ~ n telefon; ~ **call** telefoniköne; ~ **card** telefonikaart; ~ **number** telefoninumber

photo foto; ~**copy** fotokoopia; ~**graphy** fotograafia

pick up v (person) peale korjama

picnic area piknikuala

piece n tükk

Pill (birth control) rasestumisvastane tablett

pillow n padi

pink adj roosa

piste [BE] suusarada; ~ **map [BE]** suusaraja kaart

pizzeria pitsakiosk

place v (a bet) panustama

plane n lennuk

plastic wrap plastpakend

plate n taldrik

platform [BE] (train) platvorm

platinum n plaatina

play v mängima; ~ n (theatre) näidend; ~**ground** mänguväljak; ~**pen** mänguaed

please adv palun

pleasure n nauding

plunger vaakumpump

plus size plussuurus

pocket n tasku

poison n mürk

poles (skiing) suusakepp

police politsei; ~ **report** politsei aruanne; ~ **station** politseijaoskond

pond n tiik

pool n bassein

pop music popmuusika

portion n ports

post n [BE] post, ~ **office** postkontor; ~**box [BE]** postkast; ~**card** postkaart

pot n pott

pottery saviesemed

pound n (weight) nael; ~ (British sterling) nael

pregnant rase

prescribe (medication) kirjutama

prescription retsept

press v (clothing) triikima

price n hind

print v printima; ~ n trükis

problem probleem

produce n tootma; ~ **store** talupood

prohibit keelama

pronounce hääldama

Protestant protestant

public adj avalik

pull v tõmbama

purple adj lilla

purse n rahakott

push v lükkama; ~**chair [BE]** ratastool

Q

quality n kvaliteet

question n küsimus

quiet adj vaikne

R

racetrack võidusõidurada

racket n (sports) reket

railway station [BE] raudteejaam

rain n vihm; ~**coat** vihmajope; ~**forest** vihmamets; ~**y** vihmane

rap n (music) räpp

rape v vägistama; ~ n vägistamine

rare harvaesinev

rash n lööve

ravine kuristik

razor blade žiletitera

reach v ulatuma

ready valmis

real adj tegelik

receipt n tšekk

receive v saama

reception (hotel) vastuvõtt

recharge v laadima

recommend soovitama

recommendation soovitus

recycling taastöötlus

rod adj punane

refrigerator külmik

region regioon

registered mail tähitud post

regular n (fuel) tavaline

relationship suhe

rent v rentima; ~ n üür

rental car rendiauto

repair v parandama

repeat v kordama

reservation reserveering; ~ **desk** broneerimissalong

reserve (hotel) broneerima

restaurant restoran

restroom puhkeruum

retired adj (from work) pensionil

return v (something) tagastama; ~ n [BE] (trip) edasi-tagasi reis

reverse v (the charges) [BE] helistama vastuvõtja kulul

rib n (body part) ribi

right adj parem

adv (direction) paremale; ~ **of way** sõidueesõigus

ring n sõrmus

river n jõgi

road map teekaart

rob v röövima

robbed röövitud

romantic adj romantiline

room n tuba; ~ **key** toavõti; ~ **service** toateenindus

round trip edasi-tagasi reis

route n marsruut

rowboat sõudepaat
rubbing alcohol
piiritus
rubbish n [BE] prügi;
~ **bag** [BE] prügikott
rugby ragbi
ruin n varemed
rush n sööst

S

sad kurb
safe adj (protected)
turvaline; ~ n (thing)
seif
sales tax käibemaks
same adj sama
sandals sandaalid
sanitary napkin
hügieeniside
sauna saun
sauté v rasvas
praadima
save v (computer)
salvestama
savings (account)
hoiukonto
scanner skänner
scarf sall
schedule v ajas kokku
leppima; ~ n graafik
school n kool
science vaikus
scissors käärid
sea meri
seat n tool
security turvalisus
see v nägema
self-service n
iseteenindus
sell v müüma
seminar seminar
send v saatma

senior citizen
pensionär
separated (person)
lahutatud
serious tõsine
service (in a restau-
rant) teenus
sexually transmitted
disease (STD)
sugulisel teel leviv
haigus
shampoo n šampoon
sharp adj terav
shaving cream
raseerimiskreem
sheet n (bed) lina
ship v toimetama
shirt särk
shoe store kingapood
shoe king
shop v ostlema; ~ n
pood
shopping n ostlemine;
~ **area** ostupiirkond;
~ **centre** [BE]
ostukeskus; ~ **mall**
ostukeskus
short lühike;
~**-sleeved** lühikeste
varrukatega
shorts lühikesed
püksid
short-sighted [BE]
lühinägelik
shoulder n õlg
show v näitama
shower n (bath) dušš
shrine pühapaik
sick adj haige
side n külg; ~ **dish**
kõrvalroog; ~ **effect**
kõrvalmõju; ~ **order**

kõrvaltellimus
sightseeing
vaatamisväärsustega
tutvumine; ~ **tour**
vaatamisväärsuste
tuur
sign v (document)
allkirjastama
silk siid
silver n hõbe
single adj (person)
vallaline; ~ **bed**
üheinimesevoodi;
~ **print** üksiktrükk;
~ **room** ühene tuba
sink n kraanikauss
sister õde
sit v istuma
size n suurus
ski v suusatama;
~ n suusk; ~ **lift**
suusatõstuk
skin n nahk
skirt n seelik
sleep v magama; ~**er**
car magamisko-
haga auto; ~**ing bag**
magamiskott; ~**ing**
car [BE] magamisko-
haga auto
slice n viil
slippers tuhvlid
slower aeglasem
slowly aeglaselt
small väike
smoke v suitsetama
smoking (area)
suitsetamisala
snack bar snäkibaar
sneakers tennised
snowboard n
lumelaud

snowshoe n lume-
saabas
snowy lumine
soap n seep
soccer jalgpall
sock sokk
some (with singular
nouns) mõni;
~ **(with plural**
nouns) mõned
soother [BE] lutt
sore throat kur-
gupõletik
south n lõuna
souvenir n suveniir;
~ **store** suveniiripood
spa spaa
spatula spaatel
speak v rääkima
specialist (doctor)
spetsialist
specimen näidis
speeding kiiruse
ületamine
spell v kirjutama,
veerima
spicy vürtsikas;
~ **(not bland)** mitte
maitsetu
spine (body part)
selgroog
spoon n lusikas
sports sport; ~ **mas-**
sage spordimassaaž
sprain n nikastus
stadium staadium
stairs trepp
stamp v (ticket) tem-
pel; ~ n (postage)
postmark
start v alustama
starter [BE] eelroog

station n (**stop**) jaam
bus ~ bussijaam
gas ~ bensiinijaam
petrol ~ [BE] bensi-
inijaam
subway ~ metroojaam
train ~ rongijaam
statue kuju
steakhouse
liharestoran
steal v varastama
steep adj järsk
sterling silver puhas
hõbe
sting n piste
stolen varastatud
stomach kõht; ~ache
kõhuvalu
stool (bowel move-
ment) väljaheited
stop v (**bus**) peatuma;
~ n (**transportation**)
peatus
store directory (mall)
poekataloog
storey [BE] korrus
stove n ahi
straight adv (**direc-**
tion) sirgelt
strange kummaline
stream n vool
stroller (baby)
lapsekäru
student (univer-
sity) üliõpilane;
~ (**school**) õpilane
study v õpplma; ~ing n
õppimine
stuffed täidetud
stunning rabav
subtitle n subtiiter;
~ **station** jaam

suit n ülikond; ~**case**
portfell
sun n päike; ~**block**
päikesekaitse; ~**burn**
päikesepõletus;
~**glasses**
päikeseprillid; ~**ny**
päikeseline; ~**screen**
päikesevari; ~**stroke**
päikesepiste
super n (**fuel**) super;
market supermarket
surfboard lainelaud
surgical spirit [BE]
meditsiiniline piiritus
swallow v neelama
sweater sviiter
sweatshirt dres-
sipluus
sweet n [BE] maiustus;
~ adj (**taste**) magus
swelling paistetus
swim v ujuma; ~**suit**
trikoo
symbol (keyboard)
klahv
synagogue sünagoog

T

table n laud
tablet (medicine)
tablett
take v võtma
tampon n tampoon
taste v (**test**) proovima
taxi n takso
team n mccskond
teaspoon teelusikas
telephone n telefon
temple (religious)
tempel
temporary ajutine

tennis tennis
tent n telk; ~ **peg**
telgivai; ~ **pole**
telgivarras
terminal n (**airport**)
terminal
terrible kohutav
text v (**send a**
message); sõnumit
saatma ; ~ n sõnum
thank v tänama; ~ **you**
aitäh [şylle]
the (määrav artikkel)
theater teater
theft vargus
there seal
thief varas
thigh reis
thirsty janune
this see
throat kurk
thunderstorm
äiksetorm
ticket n pilet; ~ **office**
piletikassa
tie n (**clothing**) lips
tight (fit) kitsas
tights [RF] sukapüksid
time aeg; ~**table** [BE]
(**transportation**)
sõiduplaan
tire n rehv
tired väsinud
tissue kude
tobacconist
tubakakaupmees
today adv täna
toe n varvas
toenail varbaküüs
toilet [BE] tualett;
~ **paper** tualettpaber
tomorrow adv homme

tongue n keel
tonight tana
to (direction) kuhugi
tooth hammas
toothpaste hambapasta
total n (**amount**) täielik
tough adj (**food**) sitke
tour n ringkäik
tourist turist;
~ **information office**
turismiinfopunkt
tow truck puksiirauto
towel n ratik
tower n torn
town linn; ~ **hall**
raekoda; ~ **map**
linnakaart; ~ **square**
linnaväljak
toy mänguasi; ~ **store**
mänguasjapood
track n (**train**)
rongirööpad
traditional tradit-
sioonline
traffic light valgusfoor
trail n (**ski**) suusarada;
~ **map** suusaradade
kaart
trailer (car) treiler
train n rong; ~ **station**
rongijaam
transfer v (**change**
trains/flights); va-
hetama; ~ (**money**)
raha üle kandma
translate tõlkima
trash n prügi
travel n reisimine;
~ **agency** reisibüroo;
~ **sickness** mere-
haigus; ~**ers check**
[cheque BE] reisitšekk

tree puu
trim (hair) v lõikama
trip n reis
trolley [BE] (grocery
store) ostukorv;
~ [BE] (luggage)
pagas
trousers [BE] püksid
T-shirt t-särk
tumble dry trum-
melkuivatus
turn off v (device)
välja lülitama
turn on v (device)
sisse lülitama
TV televisioon
tyre [BE] rehv

U

ugly kole
umbrella vihmavari
unbranded medication
[BE] kaubamärgita
ravim
unconscious (faint)
teadvuseta
underdone toores
underground n [BE]
metroo; ~ station
[BE] metroojaam
underpants [BE]
aluspüksid
understand v aru
saama
underwear aluspesu
United Kingdom
(U.K.) Ühendkun-
ingriik
United States
(U.S.) Ameerika
Ühendriigid
university ülikool

unleaded (gas)
pliivaba
upset stomach
seedehäire
urgent kiire
urine uriin
use v kasutama
username kasuta-
janimi
utensil vahend

V

vacancy (room) vaba
tuba
vacation puhkus
vaccination vaktsiin
vacuum cleaner
tolmuimeja
vaginal infection
tupeinfektsioon
valid kehtiv
valley org
valuable adj
väärtuslik
value n väärtus
van veoauto
VAT [BE] käibemaks
vegan n veganlus;
~ adj vegan
vegetarian n
taimetoitlus; ~ adj
taimetoitlane
vehicle registration
sõiduki registreer-
imine
viewpoint (scenic)
[BE] vaade
village küla
vineyard viinapuuaed
visa viisa
visit v külastama;
~ing hours külas-

tusaeg
visually impaired
nägemispuudega
vitamin vitamiin
V-neck V-kaelus
volleyball game
võrkpallimäng
vomit v oksendama;
~ing oksendamine

W

wait v ootama; ~ n
ootus
waiter teenindaja
waiting room
ooteruum
waitress teenindaja
wake v äratama; ~-up
call äratuskõne
walk v kõndima; ~ n
jalutuskäik; ~ing
route jalutuskäigu-
rada
wallet rahakott
war memorial sõja-
line mälestusmärk
warm v (something)
soojendama; ~ adj
(temperature) soe
washing machine
pesumasin
watch v vaatama
waterfall kosk
wax v (hair) va-
hatama
weather n ilm
week nädal; ~end
nädalalõpp
weekly iganädalane
welcome adj
soovitud
you're ~ ole lahke

west n lääs
what mis
wheelchair ratastool;
~ ramp kaldtee
when adv (at what
time) millal
where kus
white adj valge;
~ gold valge kuld
who (question) kes
widowed lesestunud
wife naine (abikaasa)
window aken; ~ case
vaateaken
wine list veinikaart
wireless juhtmeta;
~ phone juhtmeta
telefon
with koos
withdraw v (money)
raha välja võtma; ~al
(bank) raha võtmine
kontolt
without ilma
woman naine
wool vill
work v töötama
wrap v pakkima
wrist ranne
write v kirjutama

Y

year aasta
yellow adj kollane
yes jah
yesterday adv eile
young adj noor
youth hostel noorte
turismibaas

Z

zoo loomaaed

ESTONIAN-ENGLISH

A

aadress address *n*

aasialik Asian *adj*

aasta year; **abi** ~ *n*

abielluma marry

ablelus married

abikaasa husband/wife

adapter adapter

advokaat lawyer *n*

aeg time

aeglaselt slowly

aeglasem slower

agentuur agency

ahi stove *n*

AIDS AIDS

ainult only

aitama help *v*

aitäh sulle thank you

ajakiri magazine

ajal during

ajalehekiosk news-
stand

ajaleht newspaper

ajas kokku leppima
schedule *v*

ajutine temporary

aken window

aktsepteerima
accept *v*

akupunktuur acu-
puncture

algaja beginner

algama begin

alkoholipood liquor
store

allahindlus discount *n*

allergiline allergic;
allergiline reakt-

sioon ~ reaction

allkirjastama sign *v*
(document)

alternatiivne marsruut
alternate route

alumiiniumfoolium
aluminium foil

aluspesu underwear

aluspüksid briefs
(clothing)

aluspüksid under-
pants [BE]

alustama start *v*

ameerika American *adj*

andma give *v*

aneemiline anemic

anesteesia anesthesia

antibiootikum
antibiotic *n*

antiikesemete pood
antiques store

antiseptiline kreem
antiseptic cream

apteek pharmacy

arkaad arcade

armas cute

armastama love *v*
(someone); **armas-**
tus ~ *n*

aroomiteraapia
aromatherapy

arst doctor *n*

arter artery

aru saama under-
stand *v*

arve invoice *n* [BE]

arvesti meter *n*
(parking)

arvuti computer

aspiriin aspirin

astmaatik asthmatic

ATM-kaart ~ card

ATM-kaart ATM

atraktsioon attraction
(place)

Austraalia Australia

austraalia Austral-
ian *adj*

auto car; **auto**
rentimine ~ rental;
autoiste ~ seat;
autorent ~ hire
[BE]; **automaatne**
automatic; **auto-**
maatkäigukastiga
auto ~ car

avalik public *adj*

avama open *v*

avar loose (fit)

avatud ~ *adj*

Ä

äiksetorm thunder-
storm

äratama wake *v*; **ära-**
tuskõne ~-up call

äravistatav dispos-
able *n*

äri business *adj*;
ärikaart ~ card;
ärikeskus ~ center;
äriklass ~ class

B

baar bar (place)

ballett ballet

bassein pool *n*

beebi baby; **beebi**
salvrätik ~ wipe;
beebipudel
~ bottle; **beebitoit**
formula (baby)

beež beige *adj*

bensiin gas (car)

bensiin petrol [BE];
bensiinijaam ~ sta-
tion; **bensiinijaam**
~ station [BE];
bensiinijaam gas
~; **bensiinijaam**
petrol ~ [BE]

bikiinid bikini

botaanikaaed botani-
cal garden

briti British *adj*

broneerima reserve
v (hotel)

broneerima reverse *v*
(the charges) [BE]

broneerimissalong
~ desk

buss bus *n*; **busse**
vahetama
~ (buses); **bus-**
sijaam ~ station;
bussijaam bus
~; **bussipeatus**
~ stop; **bussipilet**
~ ticket; **bussireis**
~ tour

C

CD CD

Celsius Celsius

D

deebetkaart debit ~:
deebetkaart debit
card
deklareerima declare
v (customs)
delikatessid delica-
tessen
deodorant deodorant
deposiit ~ n (bank)
diabeetik n
diabeetiline diabetic
adj
digitaalne digital;
digitaalne foto
~ photo; **digitaalne
kaamera** digital ~;
digitaalne kaamera
~ camera; **digitaal-
trükk** ~ print
diisel diesel
dollar dollar (U.S.)
dressipluus sweatshirt
džäss jazz n;
džässiklubi ~ club
dubleeritud dubbed
duš shower n (bath)
DVD DVD

E

edasi-tagasi reis
~ n (BE) (trip);
edasi-tagasi reis
round trip
eelroog appetizer
eelroog starter (BE)
eest for
ei no
eile yesterday adv
eine meal
e-kirja saatma e-mail
v; **e-kiri** ~ n

ekskursioon excursion
ekspert expert
ekspressbuss
express bus
ekspressrong
express train
ekstra suur ex-
tra large
elama live v; **elav
muusika** ~ music
ELi resident EU
resident
ema mother n
enne before
enne earlier
ennustus forecast n
epileptiline epileptic
adj; **epileptik** ~n
e-pilet e-ticket
e-posti aadress
e-mail address
erakorraline olukord
emergency
esimene first adj
esimene klass first
class
esimene korrus
ground floor
eskalaator escalator
euro euro

F

faks ~ n
faksi saatma fax
v; **faksinumber**
~ number
farm farm
**fikseeritud hindadega
menüü** fixed-price
menu
film film n (camera)
film movie

foto photo; **fo-
tograafia** ~graphy;
fotokoopia ~copy
föön ~ dryer

G

garaaž garage n (parking); **garaaž** ~ing
garage **autotöökoda**
~ n (for repairs)
geel gel n (hair)
gei gay adj (homosex-
ual); **geibaar** ~ bar;
geiklubi ~ club
geneeriline ravim
generic drug
giid ~ n (person)
golf golf n; **golfirada**
~ course; **golfitur-
niir** ~ tournament
graafik ~ n
gramm gram
graveerima engrave
grill barbecue
(device) n
grupp group n
günekoloog gynecolo-
gist

H

haamer hammer n
haav ~ n (injury)
habemeajaja barber
haige ill
haige sick adj
haige süda ~ condi-
tion
haiget tegema hurt v
haigla hospital
haigus cold n (sick-
ness)
halal (lubatud) halal

hall gray adj
hambaarst dentist
hambapasta
toothpaste
hammas tooth
hapnikuravi oxygen
treatment
harvaesinev rare
hea good adj; **head
päeva** ~ day
heinapalavik hay fever
hektar hectare
helistama call v
(phone); phone v
hiina Chinese adj
hiline late (time)
hind ~ (cost)
hind price n
hingama breathe
hobuserada horse-
track
hoiukapp locker
hoiukonto savings
(account)
hoki hockey
homme tomorrow adv
hommik morning n
hommikusöök
breakfast n
hoone building
hotell hotel
huul lip n
huvitav interesting
hõbe silver n
hämmastav amazing
hääldama pronounce
hügieeniside sanitary
napkin

I

ibuprofeen ibuprofen
ida east n

iganädalane weekly
igav boring
ihupiim lotion
iiri Irish *adj*
Iirimaa Ireland
iiveldav nauseous
iiveldus nausea
ilm weather *n*
ilma without
ilmutama develop *v* (film)
ilus beautiful
infopunkt ~ desk
infotelefon information-tion (phone)
inglise English *adj*
inglise keel ~ *n* (language)
insuliin insulin
Internet internet; **internetipunkt** ~ cafe; **interneti-teenus** ~ service
isa father
iseteenindus self-service *n*
iseteeninduspesuma-ja launderette [BE]
istmik buttocks
istuma sit *v*
itaalia Italian *adj*

J

jaam station *n* (stop)
jaam ~ station
jaapani Japanese *adj*
jah yes
jahe cool *adj* (temperature)
jalakäija pedestrian *n*
jalg foot *n*
jalg leg *n*

jalgpall soccer
jalgpallimäng football game [BE]
jalgratas bicycle
jalgrattatee bike route
jalutuskäigurada walking route
jalutuskäik walk *n*
janune thirsty
jeti jet ski *n*
joogimenüü drink menu
joogivesi drinking water
jook ~ *n*; **jook-sevkonto** checking account; current account [BE]
jooma drink *v*
juhataja manager
juhend guide *n* (book)
juhiloa number driver's license number
juhtkoer guide dog
juhtmeta wireless; **juhtmeta telefon** ~ phone
juuksed hair; **juuksehari** ~brush; **juukselakk** ~spray; **juukselõikus** ~cut; **juuksurisalong** ~ salon
juveliir jeweler
jõgi river
jõusaal gym *n* (place)
jäine icy
järgmine next *adj*
järsk steep *adj*
järv lake
jää ice *n*; **jäähoki** ~ hockey

K

kaamera camera; **kaamerakott** ~ case
kaart card *n*
kaart map *n*
kabaree cabaret
kadunud lost
kaebus complaint
kael neck *n*
kaelakee necklace
kaheinimesevoodi double bed
kahjustama damage *v*
kahvel fork *n*
kaldtee ~ ramp
kalju cliff
kallis expensive
kalliskivid jewelry
kallistama hug *v*
kalor calorie
kamm comb *n*
Kanada Canada
kanada Canadian *adj*
kanjon canyon
kannmikser blender
kaotama lose *v* (something)
karahvin carafe
kasiino casino
kassapidaja cashier
kasu good *n*
kasutajanimi username
kasutama use *v*
katedraal cathedral
katkine broken
kaubamaja department store
kaubamärgita ravim unbranded medication [BE]

kaubanduskeskus mall
kaugel far (distance)
kaugelenägelik far-sighted
kaugnägelik long-sighted [BE]
kauss bowl *n*
keel tongue *n*
keelama prohibit
keelduma decline *v* (credit card)
keemik chemist [BE]
keemiline puhastus dry clean; **keemiline puhastus** ~er's
keemiline tualett chemical toilet
keeruline difficult
keetma boil *v*
kehtiv valid
kena nice
kes who (question)
kesklinn downtown *n*
keskmine intermediate
keskmiselt läbipra-etud medium (steak)
kesköö midnight
kihlatud engaged (person)
kiirabi ambulance
kiire fast *adj*
kiire urgent
kiirsõnum instant message
kiiruse ületamine speeding
kiiver helmet
kile cling film [BE]
kilo kilo; **kilogramm** ~gram; **kilomeeter** ~meter

kindlustus fort
kindlustus insurance;
 kindlustuskaart
 ~ card; **kindlustus-
 selts** ~ company
king shoe
kingapood shoe store
kingipood gift shop
kink gift n
kinnine closed
kinnitama confirm
kino movie theater
kiri letter n; mail n
kirik church
kirja saatma mail v
kirjutama prescribe
 (medication)
kirjutama spell v
kirjutama write v
kitsas tight (fit)
klaas glass (drinking);
 klaas ~ (material)
klahv symbol
 (keyboard)
klass class n
klassikaline muusika
 classical music
kleit dress (clothing)
klooster monastery
klubi club n
kodumaine domestic
kogenud experienced
kohalik local n
 (person)
kohta per
kohtuma meet v
kohtumine appoint-
 ment
kohutav terrible
kohvik cafe (place)
kokkutulekusaal
 convention hall

kole ugly
kollane yellow adj
kolleeg colleague
komm candy
kondiitritoodete pood
 pastry shop
konditsioon condition
 (medical)
kondoom condom
kongestioon conges-
 tion (medical)
konservikarbiavaja
 can opener
konservtoit canned
 good
konsulaat consulate
konsultant consultant
kontaktlääts contact
 lens
konto (pangakonto)
 account n (bank)
kontor office
kontrollima check
 v (luggage);
 kontrollima ~ (on
 something)
kontsert concert;
 kontserdihall
 ~ hall
konveierilint conveyor
 belt
konverents confer-
 ence
koobas cave n
kool school n
koos with
koosolek meeting n
 (business); **koosole-
 kuruum** ~ room
kops lung
kord once (one time)
kordama repeat v

korgitser corkscrew n
koristama clean v
korrus floor n (level)
korrus storey [BE]
korter apartment
korv basket (grocery
 store)
korvpall basketball
kosk waterfall
kott bag
kraad degree
 (temperature)
kraanikauss sink n
krediitkaart credit
 card
kreem cream (oint-
 ment)
kristall crystal n
 (glass)
kude tissue
kuhugi to (direction)
kui how; **kui palju**
 ~ much
kuju statue
kuld gold n
kulmuvaha eyebrow
 wax
kummaline strange
kunst art
kunsthammas
 denture
kurb sad
kurgupõletik sore
 throat
kuristik ravine
kurk throat
kurnatud exhausted
kurt deaf adj
kus where
kustutama delete v
 (computer)
kuu month

kuulmispuudega
 hearing impaired
kuum hot (tempera-
 ture); **kuumaveeal-
 likas** ~ spring
kuupäev date n
 (calendar)
kuvar display n
 (device)
kvaliteet quality n
kõht stomach
**kõhukinnisuse
 all kannatav**
 constipated
kõhulahtisus
 diarrhea
kõhuvalu stom-
 achache
kõndima walk v
kõne call n; **kõne
 vastuvõtja kulul**
 ~ collect
kõrb desert n
kõrge high
kõrv ear; **kõrvaklapid**
 ~phones
kõrvalmõju side effect
kõrvalroog side dish
kõrvaltellimus
 side order
kõrvarõngas earring
kõrvavalu earache
kõvemini louder
käekott handbag [BE]
käevõru bracelet
käibemaks sales tax
käibemaks VAT [BE]
kämping hostel
käru cart (grocery
 store)
käsi hand n; **käsi** arm
 n (body part)

käsipagas carry-on n (piece of hand luggage)

käsipagas hand luggage

käsitsipesu hand wash

käärid scissors

köhima cough v; **köha** ~ n

köögifoolium kitchen foil [BE]

köögikombain food processor

köök kitchen

küla village

külastama visit v; **külastusaeg** ~ing hours

külg side n

külm cold adj (temperature)

külmik freezer

külmik refrigerator

külmutatud toit frozen food

küngas hill n

küpsetama bake v

küpsetama cook v

küsimus question n

küttekeha heater

küünarnukk elbow n

küünesalong nail salon

küüneviil nail file

L

laadima recharge v

lahinguväli battleground

lahkuma leave v (hotel)

lahtine kõht upset stomach

lahtiolekuaeg office hours

lahutama divorce v

lahutatud separated (person)

lainelaud surfboard

laktoositalumatu lactose intolerant

lamamistool deck chair

lamp lightbulb

valgusti light n (overhead)

laps child; **lapse ports** children's portion; **lapsehoidja** ~sitter; **lapseiste** ~'s seat; **lapsekäru** stroller (baby)

lapselaps grandchild

lastearst pediatrician

lastebassein kiddie pool

lastebassein paddling pool [BE]

lastemenüü children's menu

lastetool highchair

laud table n

leiubüroo lost-and-found

lend flight n

lennujaam airport

lennuk airplane

lennuk plane n

lennuliin airline

lennupost airmail

lesestunud widowed

lift elevator

lift lift n [BE]

ligipääs access n

liharestoran steakhouse

lihas muscle n

lihtne easy

lihunik butcher n

liiges joint n (body part)

liigesepõletik arthritis

liikmekaart membership card

liikuvus mobility

liin line n (train/bus)

liiter liter

lill flower n

lilla purple adj

lillekaupmees florist

lina linen

lina sheet n (bed)

lind bird

linn town; **linnakaart** ~ map; **linnaväljak** ~ square

lips tie n (clothing)

lisa extra adj

lisapagas excess baggage

looduskaitseala nature preserve

loom animal

loomaaed zoo

loss castle

lubama allow

lubama permit v

luksusauto luxury car

lukustama lock v; **lukk** ~ n

lumelaud snowboard n

lumesaabas snowshoe n

lumine snowy

lusikas spoon n

lutt soother [BE]

luu bone n

luud broom

lõbustuspark amuse-

ment park

lõhnavesi cologne

lõikama cut v; trim (hair) v

lõpetama end v; **lõpp** ~ n

lõug jaw n

lõuna lunch n

lõuna midday [BE]

lõuna noon n

lõuna south n

läbi reisima pass through v (travel)

läbisõit mileage

lähedal near; **lähedal** nearby

lääs west n

lääts lens

läätsevedelik contact solution

lööve rash n

lühike short; **lühikesed püksid** shorts; **lühikeste varrukatega** ~-sleeved; **lühinägelik** ~-sighted; **lühinägelik** short-sighted [BE]

lükkama push v

M

maantee highway; motorway [BE]

madal low adj

magama sleep v; **magamiskohaga auto** ~el car, **magamiskohaga auto** ~ing car [BE]; **magamiskott** ~ing bag

magus ~ adj (taste)
maha minema get off (a train/bus/subway)
maitsetu bland
maitsev delicious
maiustus sweet n [BE]
maja house n;
  majapidamistarbed ~hold goods; **majapidamisteenused** ~keeping services
majutus accommodation
maks liver (body part)
maksma cost v
maksma pay v
maksuvaba tax-free
maniküür manicure n
mantel coat
manuaalkäigukastiga auto manual car
marsruut route n
masinpestav machine washable
massaaž massage n
matkasaapad hiking boots
meditsiin medicine
meditsiiniline piiritus surgical spirit [BE]
meeldima like v
meeldiv please adv
meelelahutus entertainment
mees man (adult male)
meeskond team n
meeter ~ n (measure)
mehaanik mechanic n
menstruatsioon period (menstrual)
menstruatsiooni krambid menstrual

cramps
menüü menu (restaurant)
merehaigus motion sickness, travel sickness
meri sea
metroo underground n [BE];
  metroojaam ~ station; subway station [BE]
mets forest n
mikrolaineahi microwave n
millal when adv (at what time)
minema go v (somewhere)
minibaar mini-bar
minut minute
mis what
missa mass n (church service)
mitme reisi pilet multiple-trip ticket
mitte maitsetu spicy (not bland)
mitte miski nothing
mitte ühtegi no (not any)
mittealkohoolne non-alcoholic
mittesuitsetav non-smoking adj
mobiilne kodu mobile home
mobiiltelefon cell phone
mobiiltelefon mobile phone [BE]
mootor motor n;

mootorpaat ~ boat;
  mootorratas ~cycle
mopeed moped
mopp mop n
mošee mosque
murdma break v (bone)
must black adj
muuseum museum
muusika music;
  muusikapood ~ store
muutma alter v
mõned some (with plural nouns)
mõni some (with singular nouns)
mõõdutass measuring cup
mõõtelusikas measuring spoon
mõõtma measure v (someone)
mägi mountain;
  mägiratas ~ bike
mähe diaper; nappy [BE]
mähkmeid vahetama change v (baby)
mälestusmärk memorial (place)
mälukaart memory card
mäng game n
mängima play v;
  mänguaed ~pen;
  mänguväljak ~ground
mänguasi toy;
  mänguasjapood ~ store
münt coin

mürk poison n
müts hat
müüma sell v

N

nael pound n (weight);
  nael ~ (British sterling)
nahk leather n
nahk skin n
naine (abikaasa) wife
naine woman
nakkav contagious
nauding pleasure n
nautima enjoy
neelama swallow v
neer kidney (body part)
nikastus sprain n
nimi name n
nina nose
noor young adj
noorte turismibaas youth hostel
nuga knife
nukk doll n
number number n
numbrit valima dial v
nurga peal on the corner
nõud dishes (kitchen)
nõudepesumasin dishwasher
nõudepesuvedelik dishwashing liquid
nädal week; **nädalalõpp** ~end
nädalas per week
nägema see v
nägemispuudega visually impaired
nägemist bye
nägemist goodbye

nägu face *n*

näidend play *n* (theatre)

näidis specimen

näitama show *v*

näljane hungry

näohooldus facial *n*

närimiskumm chewing gum

nüüd now

O

odav cheap; **odav** inexpensive; **odavam** cheaper

ohtlik dangerous

OK OK

oksendama vomit *v*; **oksendamine** ~ing

ole lahke you're welcome

olema be *v*

omama have *v*

ooper opera; **ooperiteater** ~ house

ootama wait *v*; **ootus** ~ *n*; **ooteruum** ~ing room

optik optician

oranž orange *adj* (color)

org valley

orkester orchestra

osa part (for car)

ostlema shop *v*

ostlemine shopping *n*; **ostukeskus** ~ centre [BE]; **ostukeskus** ~ mall; **ostukorv** trolley [BE] (grocery store); **ostu-müügileping** bill *n* (of sale)

ostma buy *v*

ostupiirkond shopping area

otsima look *v*; **otsima midagi** ~ for something

Õ

õde nurse *n*

õde sister

õhk air *n*; **õhkkuivatus** ~-dry; **õhukonditsioneer** ~ conditioning; **õhupump** ~ pump

õhtu evening *n*

õhtusöök dinner

õlg shoulder *n*

õli oil *n*

õnnelik happy

õnnetus accident

õpilane student (school)

õppetund lesson *n*

õppima study *v*; **õppimine** ~ing *n*

Ö

öö night; **ööklubi** ~club

öömaja hommikusöögiga bed and breakfast

öös per night

P

paat boat *n*

paber paper *n* (material); **paberkäterätt** ~ towel

padi pad *n* [BE]

padi pillow *n*

pagariäri bakery

pagas luggage; baggage [BE]; **pagasi kättesaamine** ~ claim; **pagasikäru** ~ cart; **pagasilaegas** ~ locker; **pagasipilet** ~ ticket

pahkluu ankle

paikama patch *v* (clothing)

paistetus swelling

pakend carton (of groceries)

pakend package *n*

pakkima pack *v*

pakkima wrap *v*

palavik fever *n*

palee palace

palsam conditioner (hair)

paneeritud breaded

pank bank *n*

panustama place *v* (a bet)

paralleeltelefon extension (phone)

parandama fix *v* (repair)

parandama mend *v* (clothes)

parandama repair *v*

paratsetamool paracetamol [BE]

pardale astuma board *v*; **pardapääse** ~ing pass

parem better

parem right *adj*, **paremale** *adv* (direction)

parfüüm perfume *n*

parim best *adj*; **parim enne** ~ before

parkima park *v*; **park** ~ *n*; **parkimisautomaat** ~ing meter; **parkla car** ~ [BE]; **parkla** ~ing lot

parlamendihoone parliament building

pass passport; **passikontroll** ~ control

patarei battery

pea head (body part) *n*

peadpööritav dizzy *adj*

peale korjama pick up *v* (person)

peamine atraktsioon main attraction

peatuma stop *v* (bus); **peatus** ~ *n* (transportation)

peavalu headache

pediküür pedicure *n*

peenis penis

peenraha change *n* (money)

penitsilliin penicillin

pensionil retired *adj* (from work)

pensionär senior citizen

perekond family *n*

periood period (of time)

pesapall baseball

pesumaja laundromat

pesumaja laundry (place)

pesumasin washing machine

pesupesemisteenus laundry service

pidžaama pajamas

pidur brake (car)

piiritus rubbing alcohol

pikk long *adj*; **pikkade käistega** ~-sleeved

piknikuala picnic area

pilet ticket *n*; **piletikassa** ~ office

pime dark *adj*

pimesool appendix (body part)

pintsak jacket *n*

piste sting *n*

pistikupesa electric outlet

pits lace *n* (fabric)

pitsakiosk pizzeria

plaatina platinum *n*

plastpakend plastic wrap

platvorm platform [BE] (train)

pliivaba unleaded (gas)

plomm filling *n* (tooth)

pluss-suurus plus size

pluus blouse

plätud flip-flops

p.m. p.m.

poekataloog store directory (mall)

pohmell hangover

poiss boy; **poisssõber** ~friend

poksimatš boxing match

politsei police; **politsei aruanne** ~ report; **politseijaoskond** ~ station

pood shop *n*

pool half *n*; **pooleldi** half *adj*; **pool kilo** ~-kilo; **poole kohaga** ~-time *adj*; **pooltund** ~ hour

popmuusika pop music

portfell suitcase

ports portion *n*

post post *n* [BE]; **postkaart** ~card; **postkast** ~box; **postkast** ~box [BE]; **postkontor** ~ office

postmark stamp *n* (postage)

pott pot *n*

praam ferry *n*

praepann frying pan

prillid glasses

printima print *v*

probleem problem

proovikabiin fitting room

proovima taste *v* (test)

pross brooch

protestant Protestant

pruun brown *adj*

prügi rubbish *n* [BE]; **prügi** trash *n*; **prügikott** garbage bag; **prügikott** ~ bag [BE]

pudel bottle *n*; **pudeliavaja** ~ opener

puhas clean *adj* (clothes)

puhas hõbe sterling silver

puhastusvahend cleaning product

puhastusvahend

detergent

puhkeruum restroom

puhkus holiday [BE]

puhkus vacation

puksiirauto tow truck

punane red *adj*

purk jar *n* (for jam etc.)

purskkaev fountain *n*

putukas bug (insect) *n*; **putukas** insect; **putukahammustus** ~ bite; **putukatõrjevahend** ~ repellent

puu tree

puudega disabled *adj* (person); **puudega** handicapped

puuduv missing (not there)

puuetega inimeste juurdepääs handicapped-accessible

puuetega inimestele juurdepääs disabled accessible [BE]

puuvill cotton

põhi north *n*

põhikohaga full-time *adj*

põhiroog main course

põis bladder

põletama burn *v*

põlv knee *n*

päev day; **päevas** per ~

päike sun *n*; **päikesekaitse** ~block; **päikeseline** ~ny; **päikesepiste** ~stroke; **päikeseprillid** ~glasses; **päikesepõletus**

~burn; **päikesevari** ~screen

pärast after; **pärastlõuna** ~noon

pärl pearl *n*

päästevest life jacket

pühapaik shrine

püksid pants

püksid trousers [BE]

R

raamat book *n*; **raamatukogu** library; **raamatupood** ~store

rabav stunning

rada path

raekoda town hall

ragbi rugby

raha money; **raha vahetama** change (money); **raha võtmin kontolt** withdrawal (bank)

raha välja võtma withdraw *v* (money)

rahakott purse *n*

rahakott wallet

rahaks tegema cash *v*

rahatäht bill *n* (money)

rahatäht note *n* [BE] (money)

rahustaja pacifier

rahvamuusika folk music

rahvus nationality

rahvusvaheline international; **rahvusvaheline lend** ~ flight; **rahvusvaheline õpilaskaart** ~ student card

rand beach

ranne wrist

rase pregnant

raseerimiskreem shaving cream

rasestumisvastane tablett Pill (birth control)

rasvas praadima sauté v

rasvavaba fat free

ratastool wheelchair; pushchair [BE]

rattasõit cycling

raudteejaam railway station [BE]

ravi medication (drugs)

regioon region

rehv tire n

rehv tyre [BE]

reis thigh

reis trip n

reisibüroo travel agency

reisija passenger

reisimine travel n; **reisitšekk** ~ers check [cheque BE]

reket racket n (sports)

rendiauto hire car [BE]

rendiauto rental car; **rentima** hire v [BE] (a car)

rentima rent v

reserveering reservation

restoran restaurant

restorani lisatasu cover charge

retsept prescription

retseptita over-the-counter (medication)

ribi rib n (body part)

riietepood clothing store

riietumisstiil dress code

riietus clothing

riigi kood country code

rike breakdown (car)

rind breast; **rind** chest (body part)

ringkäik tour n

rinnaga toitma breastfeed v

rinnahoidja bra

rinnavalu chest pain

ristmik intersection

roheline green adj

rohkem more

romantiline romantic adj

rong train n; **rongijaam** ~ station

rongiroopad track n (train)

roosa pink adj

räpane dirty

räpp rap n (music)

rätik towel n

rääkima speak v

röövima mug v

röövima rob v

röövitud robbed

ründama attack v

S

saabas boot n

saabuma arrive

saabumine arrival

saadaval available

saama receive v

saastatud infected

saatma send v

saksa German adj; **saksa keel** ~ n (language)

Saksamaa Germany

salasõna password

salgud highlights (hair)

sall scarf

salvestama save v (computer)

salvrätt napkin

sama same adj

sandaalid loafers

sandaalid sandals

saun sauna

saviesemed pottery

seaduslik kosher adj

seal there

see this

seedekulgla intestine

seelik skirt n

seep soap n

sees in

seif safe n (thing)

seksima have sex

selg back (body part)

selgesõnaline express adj

selgroog spine (body part)

seljakott backpack

seljavalu backache

seminar seminar

sentimeeter centimeter

side bandage

sigar cigar

sigaretipakk carton (of cigarettes)

siid silk

siin here

sild bridge

silm eye

sinine blue adj

sirge kaelus crew neck

sirgelt straight adv (direction)

sisaldama include v

sisebassein indoor pool (public)

sisenema enter v (place)

sisestama insert v (card)

sisse logima log on v (computer)

sisse lülitama turn on v (device)

sissemaksu tegema deposit v (money)

sissemurdmine break-in (burglary) n

sissepääs entrance

sisseregistreerimine check-in

sitke tough adj (food)

skänner scanner

snäkibaar snack bar

soe warm adj (temperature); **soe vesi** ~ water; **soojendamine** ~ing [BE]

soeng hairstyle

sokk sock

soojendama heat v; warm v (something)

soovitama recommend

soovitatav hind around (price)

soovitud welcome adj

soovitus recommendation
spaa spa
spaatel spatula
spetsialist specialist (doctor)
sport sports; **spordimassaaž** ~ massage
staadium stadium
stilist hair stylist
subtiiter subtitle *n*
sugulisel teel leviv haigus sexually transmitted disease (STD)
suhe relationship
suitsetama smoke *v*
suitsetamisala smoking (area)
sukapüksid tights [BE]
sukelduma dive *v*
sukeldumisvarustus diving equipment
sukkpüksid pantyhose
sularaha cash *n*; **sularahaautomaat** ATM
sulepea pen *n*
sulgema close *v* (a shop)
super super *n* (fuel); **supermarket** ~market
suu mouth *n*
suudlema kiss *v*
suunakood area code
suund direction
suur big; **suur** large; **suurem** bigger
suurepärane magnificent

suurus size *n*
suusakepp poles (skiing)
suusarada piste [BE]; **suusarada** trail *n* (ski); **suusaradade kaart** ~ map; **suusaraja kaart** ~ map [BE]
suusatama ski *v*
suusatõstuk drag lift
suusatõstuk ski lift
suusatõstuki pilet ski lift pass
suusk ski *n*
suveniir souvenir *n*; **suveniiripood** ~ store
sviiter sweater
sõber friend
sõel colander
sõidueesõigus right of way
sõiduki registreerimine vehicle registration
sõiduplaan timetable [BE] (transportation)
sõitma drive *v*
sõjaline mälestusmärk war memorial
sõnum message; text ~ *n*
sõnumit saatma text *v* (send a message)
sõrm finger *n*; **sõrmeküüs** ~nail
sõrmus ring *n*
sõudepaat rowboat
säritus exposure (film)
särk shirt

söögipulgad chopsticks
söögituba dining room
sööma eat *v*
sööst rush *v*
süda heart
sügav deep *adj*
sünagoog synagogue
sünnipäev birthday
šampoon shampoo *n*

T

taastöötlus recycling
tablett tablet (medicine)
taga behind (direction)
tagastama return *v* (something)
taimetoitlus vegetarian *n*; **taimetoitlane** ~ *adj*
takso taxi *n*
taldrik plate *n*
talupood produce store
tampoon tampon *n*
tankima fill *v* (car)
tantsima dance *v*; **tantsimine** ~ing; **tantsuklubi** ~ club
tasku pocket *n*
taskulamp flashlight
tass cup *n*
tasu fee *n*
tasu võtma charge *v* (credit card)
tavaline regular *n* (fuel)
teadvuseta unconscious (faint)
teater theater
teavitama notify *v*

teekaart road map
teelusikas teaspoon
teemant diamond
teenindaja waiter
teenindaja waitress
teenus service (in a restaurant)
tegelik real *adj*
tekk blanket
teksad jeans
teksasriie denim
telefon phone *n*; **telefon** telephone *n*; **telefoniautomaat** pay~; **telefonikaart** ~ card; **telefonikõne** ~ call; **telefoninumber** ~ number
televisioon TV
telgi põhi groundcloth
telgivai tent peg
telgivarras tent pole
telk tent *n*; **telkima** camp *v*; **telkimisplats** ~site; **telkimispliit** ~ing stove
tellimus order *v* (restaurant)
tempel stamp *v* (ticket)
tempel temple (religious)
tennis tennis
tennised sneakers
terav sharp *adj*
tere hello
tere hi
tere hommikust good morning; **tere päevast** good afternoon; **tere õhtust** good evening

terminal terminal *n* (airport)

tervis health

Terviseks! Cheers!

tervisliku toidu pood health food store

tiik pond *n*

tikk match *n*

tilguti drop *n* (medicine)

tinasulam pewter

tipp peak *n* (of a mountain)

toateenindus room service

toavõti room key

toidupood grocery store

toimetama ship *v*

toit food; **toitma** feed *v*

toll customs

tollimaks duty (tax)

tolmuimeja vacuum cleaner

tool chair *n*

tool seat *n*

tooma bring

toores underdone

tootma produce *n*

torn tower *n*

tosin dozen

traditsiooniline traditional

trahv fine *n* (fee for breaking law)

treiler trailer (car)

trepp stairs

triikima iron *v*

triikima press *v* (clothing)

triikraud iron *n* (clothes)

trikoo swimsuit

trummelkuivatus tumble dry

trükis print *n*

t-särk T-shirt

tšekk receipt *n*

tualett toilet [BE]; **tualettpaber** ~ paper

tualettvesi aftershave

tuba room *n*

tubakakaupmees tobacconist

tuhvlid slippers

tulekindel uks fire door

tulema come *v*

tuletõrje fire department

tuli fire *n*; **tuli** light *n* (cigarette)

tund hour

tunnis per hour

tunnistus certificate

tunnus identification

tupeinfektsioon vaginal infection

turg market *n*

turismiin- fopunkt tourist information office

turist tourist

turistiklass economy; economy class

turvaline safe *adj* (protected)

turvalisus security

tutvustama introduce *v* (person)

tõlk interpreter

tõlkima translate

tõmbama pull *v*

tõsine serious

tõstuk cable car

tõstuk chairlift

tõstuk lift *n* (ride)

tähitud post registered mail

täidetud stuffed

täielik total *n* (amount)

täitma fill out *v* (form)

täna today *adv*

täna tonight

tänama thank *v*

töötama work *v*

tüdruk girl; **tüdruk- sõber** ~friend

tühistama cancel

tühjendama empty *v*

tükk piece *n*

tüütama bother *v*

U

ujuma swim *v*

uks door

ulatuma reach *v*

unetus insomnia

unisus drowsiness

uriin urine

uustulnuk novice

Ü

ühe otsa pilet (buss, rong, metroo) (bus/ train/subway); **ühe otsa pilet (lennuk)** one-way ticket (airline)

ühe päeva pilet one-day (ticket)

üheinimesevoodi single bed

ühekordsell kasutatav raseerija disposable razor

ühendama connect (internet)

Ühendkuningriik United Kingdom (U.K.)

Ühendriigid United States (U.S.)

ühendus connection (travel/internet); **uhenduslend** connection flight

ühendust võtma contact *v*

ühene tuba single room

ühesuunaline tänav one-way street

ühinema join *v* (go with somebody)

ühiselamu dormitory

üks one; (counting)

üksiktrükk single print

üksinda alone

üle over *prep* (direction); **üleku- umenenud** ~heat *v* (car); **ülepraetud** ~done (meat); **üleöö** ~night

ülikond suit *n*

ülikool university

üliõpilane student (university)

ümber (nurga) around (the corner)

ümber keha riided fit *n* (clothing)

ümbrik envelope
üür rent

V

vaade overlook *n* (scenic place); **vaade** viewpoint (scenic) [BE]
vaakumpump plunger
vaatama watch *v*
vaatamisväärsuste tuur sightseeing tour
vaatamisväärsustega tutvumine sightseeing
vaateaken window case
vaba free *adj*
vaba tuba vacancy (room)
vabakutseline töötaja freelance work
vabandama excuse *v*
vahatama wax *v* (hair)
vahekäigupoolne koht aisle seat
vahekäik aisle
vahend utensil
vahetama transfer *v* (change trains/flights)
vahetus exchange *v*; **vahetuskurss** ~ rate
vaht mousse (hair)
vaikne quiet *adj*
vaikus science
vajama need *v*
vaktsiin vaccination
valge white *adj*; **valge kuld** ~ gold

valgusfoor traffic light
vallaline single *adj* (person)
valmis ready
valu pain
valuuta currency; **valuutavahetus** ~ exchange; **valuuta-vahetuspunkt** ~ exchange office
valuutavahetuspunkt exchange *n* (place)
vana old *adj*
vanavanemad grandparents
vannituba bathroom
vanus age *n*
varajane early
varas thief
varastama steal *v*
varastatud stolen
varbaküüs toenail
varemed ruin *n*
vargus theft
varustus equipment
varuväljapääs emergency exit
varvas toe *n*
vasak left *adj, adv* (direction)
vask copper *n*
vastand opposite *n*
vastuvõtt reception (hotel)
vastuvõtt (hind) admission (price)
veetlev attractive
veganlus vegan *n*; **vegan** ~ *adj*
veinikaart wine list
veinipood off-licence [BE]

vend brother
ventilaator fan *n* (appliance)
veoauto van
vererõhk blood pressure
veri blood
veritsema bleed
vetelpäästja lifeguard
viga mistake *n*
vihm rain *n*; **vihmajope** ~coat; **vihmamets** ~forest; **vihmane** ~y
vihmavari umbrella
viil slice *n*
viimane last *adj*
viinapuuaed vineyard
viisa visa
viivitama delay *v*
vill wool
vitmiin vitamin
vitriin display case
V-kaelus V-neck
voodi bed *n*
vool stream *n*
vorm form *n* (document)
võidusõidurada racetrack
võlga tasuma clear *v* (on an ATM)
võrevoodi crib
võrkpallimäng volleyball game
võte/võtted take ~s
võti key *n*
võtma take *v*
võtmehoidja keyring
võtmekaart key card
vägistama rape *v*; **vägistamine** ~ *n*

vähem less
väike little
väike small
välgu kasutamine pildistamiseks flash photography
välgumihkel lighter *n*
välibassein outdoor pool
välja astuma leave (plane)
välja logima log off *v* (computer)
välja lülitama disconnect (computer)
välja lülitama turn off *v* (device)
välja tõmbama extract *v* (tooth)
väljaheited stool (bowel movement)
väljak field (sports)
väljapääs exit *n*
väljaregistreerimine check-out
väljas outside *prep*
väljasõit departure (plane)
väljuma exit *v*
värav gate (airport)
värske fresh
värv color *n*
väsinud tired
väärtus value *n*
väärtuslik valuable *adj*
vöö belt
vürtsikas hot (spicy); **vürtsikas** spicy

Z

žiletitera razor blade

INDEX

Berlitz pocket guide

Special Sales, Content Licensing and CoPublishing

...des can be purchased in bulk
...t discounted prices. We can
...ial editions, personalised jackets
...ate imprints tailored to your
...s@insightguides.com;
...tguides.biz

...eserved
... Digital [CH] AG and
...tions [UK] Ltd

...hina by CTPS

...his book may be reproduced,
...etrieval system or transmitted in
... means electronic, mechanical,
...g, recording or otherwise,
...r written permission from Apa

...has been made to provide
...ormation in this publication,
...are inevitable. The publisher
...ponsible for any resulting loss,
...e or injury. We would appreciate
...would call our attention to any
...dated information. We also
...r suggestions; please contact
...@apaguide.co.uk
...guides.com/berlitz

...mark Reg. U.S. Patent Office
...untries. Marca Registrada.
...cence from the Berlitz
...orporation